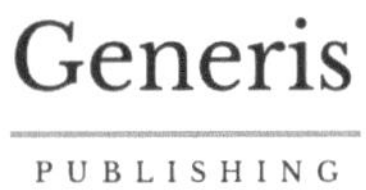

Generis

PUBLISHING

Designing for Placebo:
On the Sleeve Arts of the Band Placebo
Vol.1, 1995-2000

Cinla SEKER, Ph.D

CIP a Camerei Naţionale a Cărţii

Seker, Cinla.

Designing for Placebo: On the Sleeve Arts of the Band Placebo / Cinla Seker. – Chişinău : Generis Publishing, 2020 (Print on demand) – ISBN 978-9975-154-20-8
Vol. 1 : 1995-2000. – 2020. – 69 p. : fig. – Referinţe bibliogr.: p. 63-68.
7.05:78 S 42

Cover image: www.pixabay.com

Generis Publishing

Online orders: www.generis-publishing.com

Orders by email: info@generis-publishing.com

Prologue

Album cover design / sleeve art is a sub-area of graphic design, which deals with type and images on two-dimensional limited surfaces of any kind. From the 19th Century music documented since the invention of the recording techniques, which allow the listener to hear it as performed. The fragility of the music recorded mediums concluded in different types of wrapping by different types of material. Technology was determinative on recording mediums both in and out like in every creative act in anytime anywhere. While recording techniques improving, mediums have changed so the packages… (Heller & Fernandes, 2010: 99; Morton Jr, 2004: ix-x)

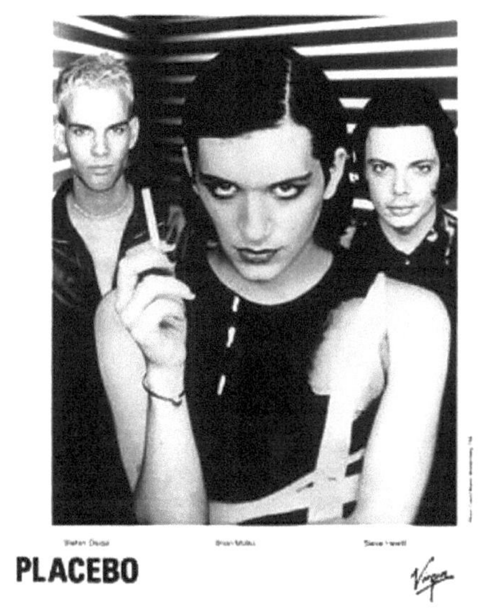

Figure 1. One of the iconic photos of the band Placebo,

Author's collection

Initially besides protection and storing, the classification of these music recorded mediums also needed. The packages typed, enumerated, and finally illustrated, which was a must-do for marketing from the beginning of the music's mass production era and so on (Meggs & Purvis, 2016: 477). Graphically designed packages have used the visual elements of fine arts - today visual arts- according to their own principles: graphic design principles, which some similar some so different than the principles of fine arts (Poulin, 2012: 6-7). Based on Bauhaus of the early 20th Century these principles were blende by the needs of the marketing (Droste, 2002: 6-7). This marketing had meant beyond selling for a musician, who expresses itself by his / her music as an artistic outcome and wants to reach masses to be understood as a basic need.

A square formatted surface visually designed for representing the music behind, which is audial based on sound and silence now expressed visually on this graphic space. In the hundred years of this journey there are some typographic samples without any image and there were also samples using visuals only in a form of an iconic photograph or a simple black surface but nothing. When examined in detail it has been always approved that there is a close form and content relation with these albums covers / sleeve piece of arts and the music they are representing and the musician's self as a musical artist. In this special instance, starring the band Placebo, uncovered by analyzing the covers of their studio, live, compilations, EP's, and single albums to the year 2000.

English rock band formed in 1994 in London. Since the first album release, the first wave post-punk bands they are compared like Sonic Youth, Depeche Mode, the Cure, early U2 and Talking Heads. All along the 26 years with their 7 studio albums all in Top 20 in UK, and with their 2 live, 9 compilations, 6 EPs, 33 single albums, it is obvious that they responded a precious need in the Britpop scene and worldwide with their 11 million records. Until 2017 they had nominated for 30 prestigious music awards worldwide and won the 4: the group of the year in 2004, classic songwriter of the year in 2006, best alternative music of the year in 2009 and the artist's artist award of the year in 2015. (Cogan, 2006: 104; Gregory, 2002: 318; Larkin, 2006: 563; Strong, 1998: 629; www.themmf.net)

Characterized with the distinctive nasal, high-pitched vocal of Brian Molko and his aggressive guitar and unique tunings, Placebo has tense, fast - rocking songs with clearly articulated guitar riffs, heavy bass grooves, busy drumming performed by bassist - guitarist Stefan Olsdal, and replacing drummers like Robert Schultzberg, Steve Hewitt, and Steve Forrest (www.trouserpress.com). Throughout their career, Placebo's sound described by the music critics under the alternative rock umbrella as progressive rock – grunge – punk rock in early works; but pop punk, industrial rock, Britpop, glam rock, gothic rock, electronic rock, post-punk revival, and experimental rock in general. From the content and lyrical perspective, sexuality, mental health, and drug use themes within a combination of androgynous appearance with visual onstage LGBT messages made Placebo a gender-bending band. (Buckley, 2003: 1033)

On the Sleeve Arts

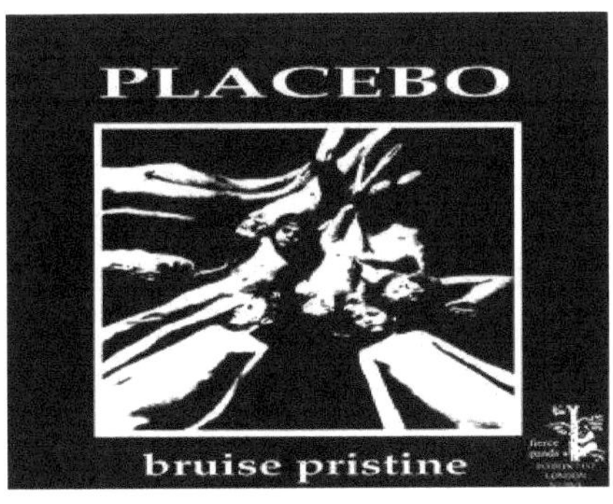

Figure 2. Bruise pristine 1995 release cover, *Author's collection*

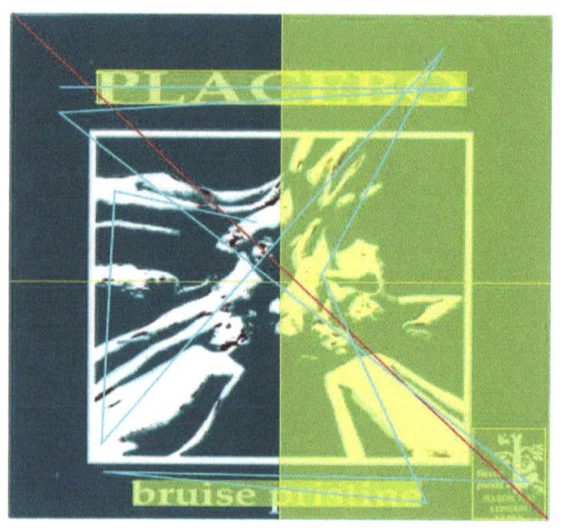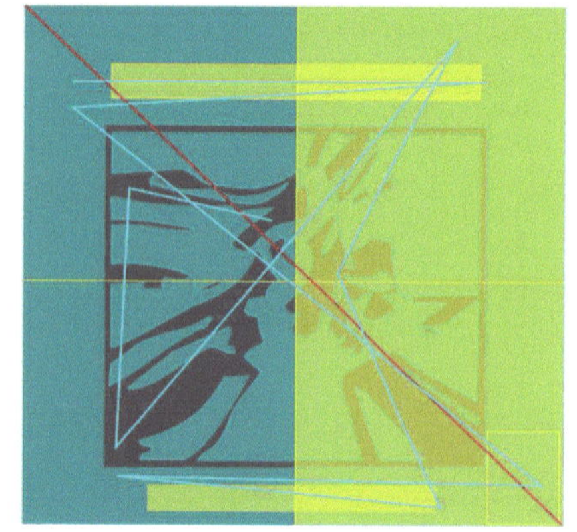

Figure 3. Bruise pristine 1995 release cover's formal analysis, *by Seker*

The very first single album of the band Placebo *Bruise pristine* released in 1995 and labeled as alternative rock, which is indicating a separation from mainstream (Thompson, 2010: 159). Heavy riff within a combination of behind the bridge guitar solo and dark lyrics performed by Molko's soulful voice reflected on the highly contrasting monochromatic album cover. Naked group of figures seen as a distorted odd photograph reduced into only two tones: black & white, which can be perceived as a reflection of sad and negative feelings. These naked figures are the primitive samples of the artistic nude photography canon, which is going to last for more than two decades with exceptions. No greys left to make the figures rigid and sharp. With the help of the deformation in shape and value the image turned into an abstract composition, which diagonal and asymmetrically balanced. This kind of a composition makes the image vivid, vibrant, and dynamic. For a debut release the name of the band and the music placed on top and on the bottom of the cover in huge sizes to be seen and red easily. For the name of the band a typeface in average line thicknesses chosen. Both the style of the typeface and white uppercases on black background help to emphasize the name of the band. A similar typeface has chosen for the name of the release but in lowercases this time and placed under the image. It is a hybrid typeface because of its serifs and stable line thicknesses. Although the diagonal composition of the image, the types almost justified. It is because a fourth element, the logotype of the recording company in white placed on right bottom balance the diagonal asymmetrical composition of the image. While these rough characteristics of the cover suits to the hard style of the music but contradicts with the high sensuousness lays under. Dynamism on a two-dimensional surface created by using irregular shapes in different sizes and distributed to the surface asymmetrically. An asymmetrically balanced composition examined by dividing the surface into two halves both horizontally and vertically to see whether the two halves are reflecting each other as shape and color. The rigid white frame surrounding by pitch black the image used as an organizational separator in between the overcrowded image.

Come home released in 1996 labeled as pop punk under alternative rock umbrella indicating the combination of up-tempo punk rock moods with power pop harmonies (www.discogs.com). While the melodic hooks, vocal harmonies, an energetic performance and a so called happy sound underpinned by yearning, longing and despair are the characteristics of these power pop harmonies, short, fast-paced songs with hard-edged melodies and a hard-edged vocal style, stripped down instrumentation and anti-establishment lyrics are the characteristics of punk rock. From these definitions it is obvious to see that in both genres pain and tragedy are leading characters melted in each other reflected as two parted life vests in red. The proportions of the two parts and positioning of the plugs like nipples in the human body perceived by the viewer like burning lungs with blurred outlines in black. This can be accepted as a new form of transparency and nudity used another object to identify. Despite the stable symmetrical installation of the vest the vivid red surrounded and digs by the strong black, the creamy white symbols and lettering on the curves of inflation makes the cover dynamic and alive. It is also shocking as a photographic theme for a musical release cover, but it is also understandable for an artistic production based on expressing the very deep feelings and ideas.

On the search for a suitable typeface for both the name of the band and the music a font chosen thinner, plain, and suitable with the visual aspects of the image. The character used has regular geometric features like curves with the proportions of a perfect circle seen on left halve of the vest and 90 degrees ascenders which are vertical suited to the perfectness of the whole cover as a square. The repetition as a design element used all over the cover in the form of proportion 1:1, which is a proportion of a square and a circle repeating as the cover itself, the two pieced vest, the creamy circle on left, the two circles of the two plugs and finally lowercase letters. The second organization to asymmetrically balance the cover is the placements of the two letter groups, one on top left and the other on bottom right, which balances the flying circular symbol and the triangular top corners and slightly angular bottoms of the two parts of the vest. The band's name placed on top in bigger size is useful on this very second release for presentational purposes. The letters have two dimensions, which are sending the verbal message and beings which have special shape, colors, size, and locations. The creamy white color of the letters guaranteed both the legibility in front of a dark background and to be a part of the color scheme to create a harmony and unity among the visuals.

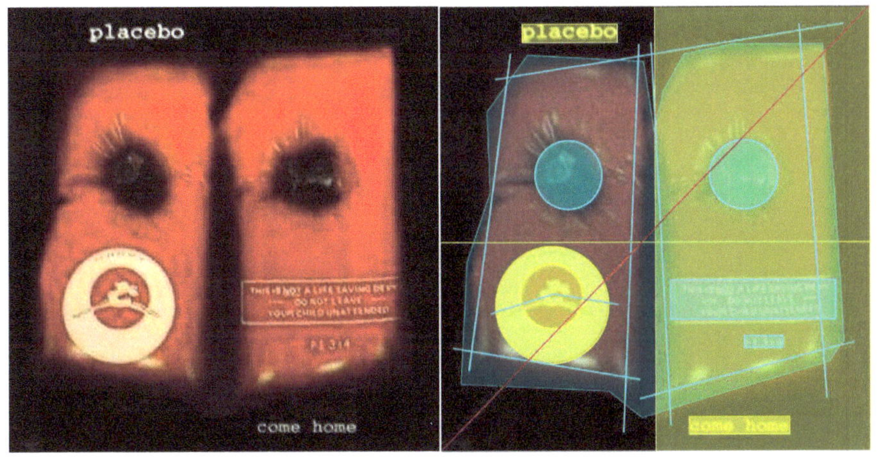

Figure 4. Come home release cover, Author's collection

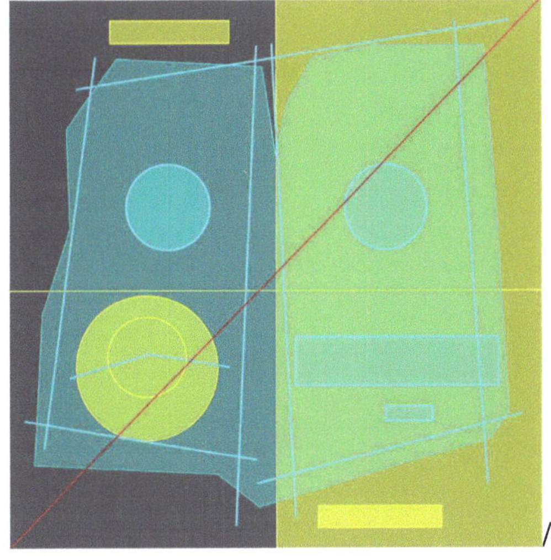

Figure 5. Come home release cover's formal analysis, *by Seker*

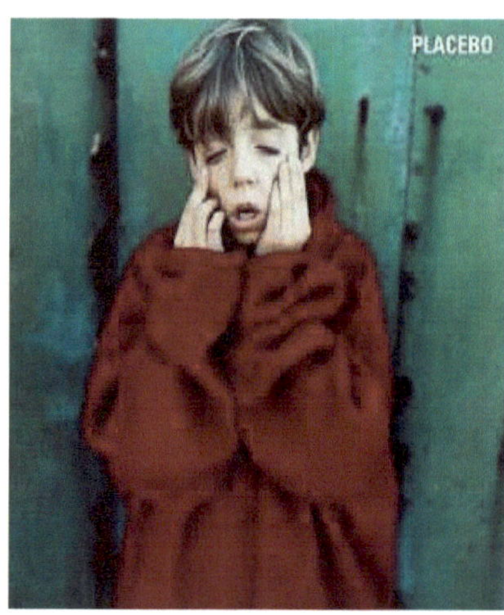

Figure 6. Placebo release cover, *Author's collection*

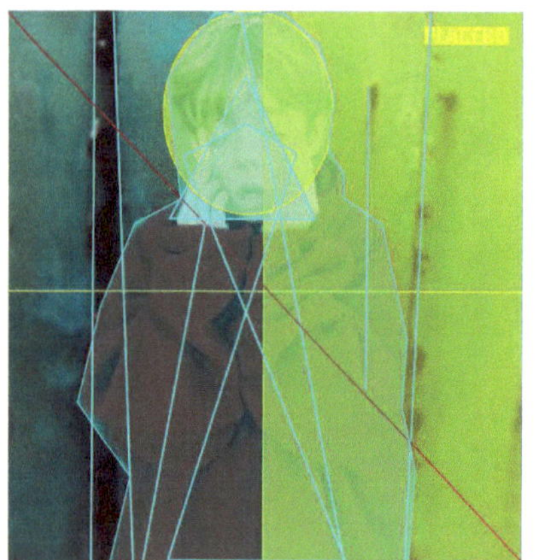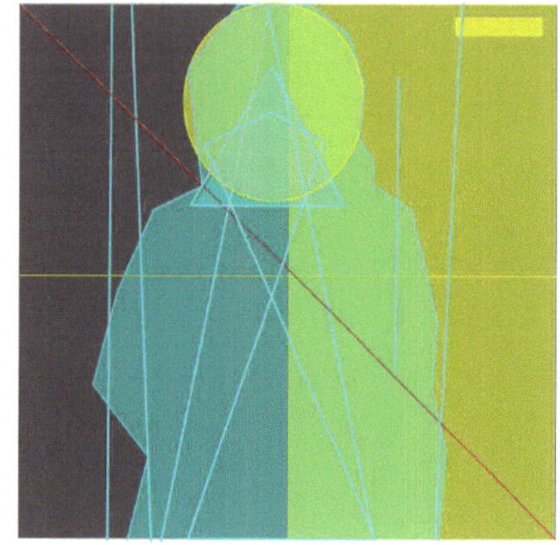

Figure 7. Placebo release cover's formal analysis, *by Seker*

The first studio album of the Placebo released in 1996 *Placebo* carried the photographic album cover canon with a real-life photograph of a ten years old boy crying (www.allmusic.com). Real life photography captured the real-life scene as it is seen in real (Shaffer & Shaffer, 2019: 69). A blond boy crying within a bigger size bright red cardigan standing in front of a turquoise scratched background. Striking red life vest of the previous release cover has turned into a large size cardigan with its curvy inflations melted in black, has two symmetrical sides and look like it is burning inside but standing still. The pain that wanted to express is supported and proved by the real cry on the child's face, although he is trying to hide with his both hands and by hiding behind this turquoise something. The most contrasting color of this bright red on the color wheel is this kind of turquoise which lays in just the opposite (Bleicher, 2012: 72). This means after black and white, which are not colors but tones, the most contrasting color is used as a background within a combination in black and creamy yellowish whites. The opposites in colors are also complementary, when they used in combination, they are harmonious according to the color harmonies system, which tries to find color combinations aesthetically pleasing (Holzschlag, 2003: 38-40).

Slightly left turning head of the boy and barely seen asymmetries in his body as pose and in the background as textural details balanced by the placement of the modern sans serif typeface used to write the band's name on top right (Squire, Forssman & Willberg, 2006: 18). Visual asymmetries like in real life balances, when a movement or an entity point a direction with its position, an opposite movement or entity placed to asymmetrically balance the visual composition concluded in dynamism and stress, which is expressive and aesthetically pleasing. Searching for the name of the album concluded in finding out that they are the same. When examined in detail it is easily be seen that the proportions of every letter typed in uppercases are the same proportion of the boy as a figure. This plain but powerful typeface gives the designer to type it as small as it can be but still legible, which was asked by the band members.

The *36 degrees* released in 1996 with another real-life photographic image on its cover (www.allmusic.com). Although it is real life this time there is nothing but the creamy white skin colors in a combination with white and dark cream tones as shadows. A transparent plastic wrapped left hand seen in the middle of the surface falls almost in a freeway. On plain cream background textured as a regular indoor wall, two thin white cables accompany the hand the way it moves: one along with the hand, other aside going down. These thin white cables resemble delicate electronic equipment of the hospitals, when combined pale colors, plain space and thin transparent plastic wrap. When examining in detail, it is easily seen that all three singles in this release are related to unrequited love theme. The name given first song's narrator is nearly dying of his/her love. The second song, which is a cover of a love song by the founder member of the famous rock band Pink Floyd, Syd Barret, who's life disrupted by mental illnesses caused by drugs and turned into a failure (De Barres, 1996: 1-9; Fielder, 2013: 219). Handsome, creative, and talented prospective rock star was suffering from a lonesome poverty. The last song of the release is keep telling the great mantra of Hare Krishna, dedicated to the supreme Hindu God Krishna, which is the God of compassion, tenderness and love; Krishna always depicted as a young beautiful boy with his blue skin while playing a flute (Nuit, 2015: 23). Barret's black and white photograph showed him while meditating and the name of the very first album of Pink Floyd from times Barret was a member of the band was *The piper at the gates of dawn*, which is a quote from the Kenneth Graham story *The wind in the willows* (Ellis, 2012: 44). In a scene the ancient Greek mythological God Pan occurs and shows the characters of the story the way with his enchanting music; as a God of nature, wild mountains, shepherds and flocks Pan is often associated with sexuality (Edgar, 2008: 5). While Pan is a hybrid form of man and goat, Krishna has a blue skin and female beauty in man body.

While the blue color of Krishna's skin is indicating all-inclusiveness like the sky and sea for Indians and East, it is the color of dead body in West.

The main character nearly dying of love and suffocation of his unrequited love symbolized by the image, which continues the nudity cannon and multiply it with real nudity and nude coloring consists pale skin tone, cream and white. This nudity also exists both in Barret / Pink Floyd's photographs, release covers, and Greek / Hindu pieces of artworks related with Pan and Krishna. The name of the band and release typed as small as they are legible still. By not taking the attention on them by being white, small, and plain separated by a comma to differentiate and determinate. Placing on top right on a horizontal line side by side asymmetrically balanced the down going movements and directions of the hand and the two cables.

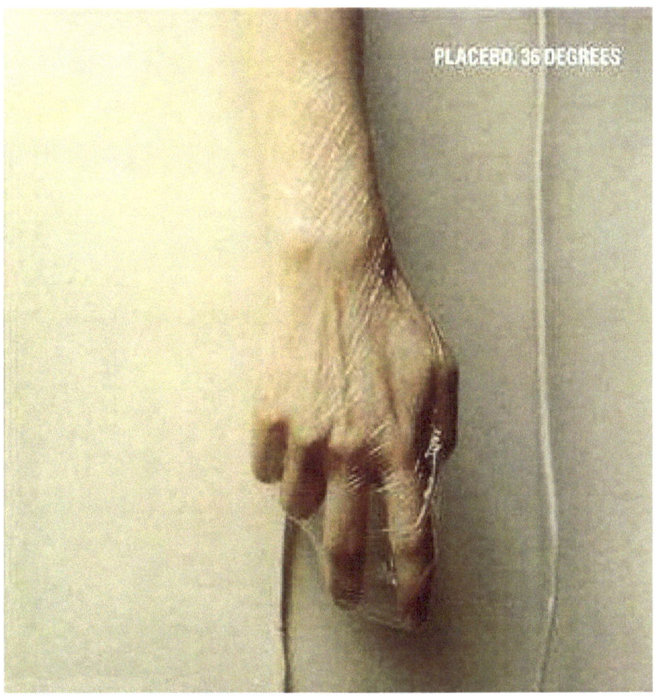

Figure 8. 36 degrees release cover, *Author's collection*

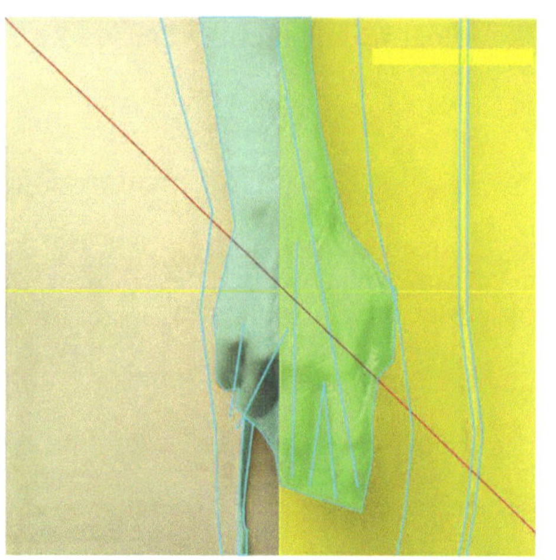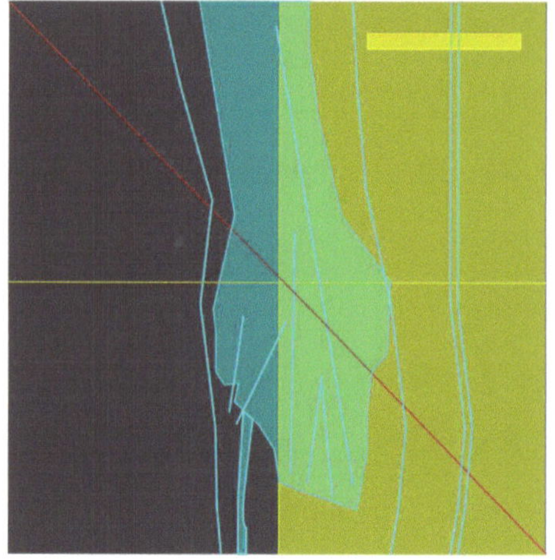

Figure 9. 36 degrees release cover's formal analysis, *by Seker*

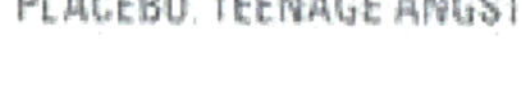

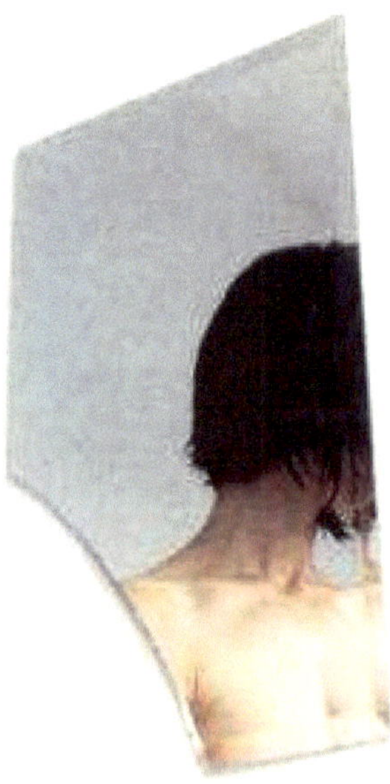

Figure 10. Teenage angst release cover, *Author's collection*

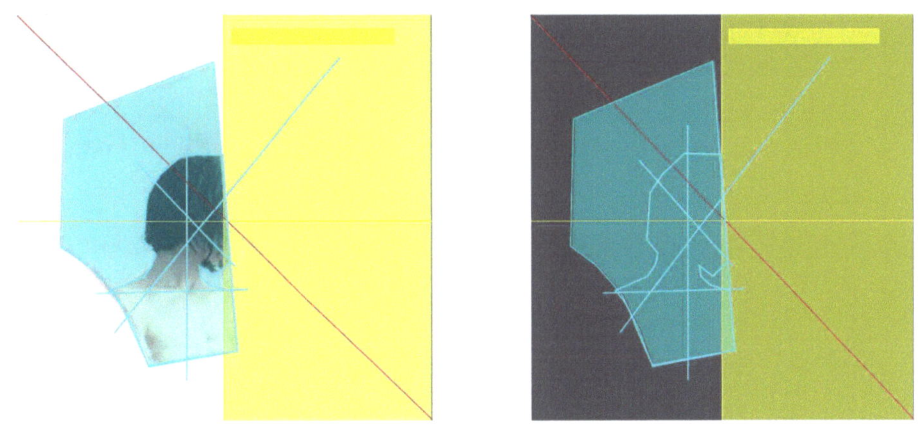

Figure 11. Teenage angst release cover's formal analysis, *by Seker*

Same year in the September *Teenage angst* released labeled as same genre as alternative rock (Valentine, 2017: 282). After the name given song, the *Been smoking too long* seen in form of Nick Drake cover, which originally is an anonymous song (Wiseman-Trowse, 2013: 48). Drake was an English singer-song writer of folk music, who died young and appreciated decades after his death caused by suffering from mental illness and drug use (Talevski, 2006: 142-143). Second folk revival, which reached its zenith in the 60s (Shepherd, Horn, Laing, Oliver & Wicke (Eds.), 2003: 348), overlaps the teenage and ongoing years of Drake. A male figure, which has long hair and white skin like Drake in a broken mirror on the cover of the release, is also something incomplete. Mirror in visual arts used since 15th Century in Europe. *Venus effect* called to such artworks, in which half naked female figures accepted as admiring their own beauty, depicted as looking at the painter / viewer from the mirror (Shapiro & Todorovic, 2017: 611). Goddess of love, beauty, desire, fertility, and prosperity Roman Venus – Aphrodite in Greek- gave its name to this tradition (Sonak, 2017: 186). Despite being naked, the figure in the mirror on the cover assumed as male because of the structural body, looked to somewhere else and physically identified only because of its hidden face. With this figure the nude cannon continues. The mirror is not broken; it is cut out on purpose carefully. It is like turning around the still standing figure with its angular sides and curvy cutout corner in the bottom. Like the organic shape of the figure, the cutout mirror also has a unique and irregular frame. Placed as it covers the left half of the cover the cutout mirror with its angles leads the eye to the bottom half of the surface. This movement asymmetrically balanced by placing the name of the band and the release on top right as a line by using the same typeface in approximately similar size like the previous two covers. Pale greyish sky behind the figure in the mirror is the color of these names both placed on white surface by using a touch of shadow effect, which confused the viewer about the figure - ground relationship. Figure - ground is a basic principle used in visual arts rooted in visual perception rules (Arnheim, 1974: 228). Like in real life the viewer expects to see a figure in front of a background. A joyful illusion made to change this rule by adding a shadow under a mirror and turn it into a figure. A mirror with a depth effect inside confuses the mind and makes the cover dynamic, which is interesting and alive. Pale coloring by using no color on the cover convince the viewer in a consistent color scheme using for cover designs. The tones used called neutral colors, which are low saturated like seen in the sky on the mirror. The sky is not blue anymore, it is a light grey made by reducing all the hue and adding some light. On a design color is a powerful tool, which affects the viewer by sending warm, energetic, and cheerful messages, when they are vivid and bright. Or just the opposite by using pale or dark neutrals like black, brown and greys. Although white relaxes the eye it should remind the viewer that it is not a color, it is a state of emptiness.

By the New Year in January 1997 *Nancy Boy* released in two parts titled *Part 1 of 2* and *Part 2 of 2*, labeled as genre grunge and Britpop besides alternative rock (Larkin, 2000: 312). While grunge rooted in United States' rock scene of Seattle in mid 1980s, Britpop occurred after a decade in UK; while grunge fuses the elements of punk rock with heavy metal and also influenced by the indie rock bands, Britpop on the other hand, with its brightness and catchier music emphasized Britishness by using the same instruments with each other (Berger, 2012: 34-35; Hawkins, 2017: 52). Like in the previous single releases this release has a cover, a cover of the song *Bigmouth strikes again* of the English rock band *The Smiths* (Wild (Ed.), 2009: 29). Short lived but one of the most important bands The Smiths has an aesthetic simplicity as a reaction to New Romantics' excessive outfit but still androgynous combined with casualty (Lime, 2019: 27). Has lyrics black humor, self-deprecating, and pop vernacular in combination with drama, sexuality, and violence like the "smashing teeth" in *Bigmouth strikes again* (Goddard, 2009: 32). On all their release covers -approximately 55- monochrome photographs of cult films, actors and pop stars; figures from 1960s British pop culture; and anonymous old film and magazines used. Most of them only have the band's name, the rest combined with minimized album names. A coincidence seen among the *Nancy boy* release set and 1992 released *The Smiths Best I...* and *...Best II* release sets, which is a young man half naked with some tattoos (www.nme.com). What a coincidence the covered song of The Smiths is also placed inside the *...Best II* as number eight in the track listing. Almost black & white, low saturated photography used on *Nancy boy*, natural white skin placed in a white environment in a combination with some light shades, tattoo tones and natural denim. The color scheme, transparent nudity and typographic style canon continues throughout the design. The plain, simple, sans serif *Placebo* typeface used as same size, tone and as a line with the name of the release placed on top right contrasting with the huge emptiness in the ground as proportional size. This placement asymmetrically balanced the diagonal composition built by cutting the figure out and placing it down left corner. Extraordinary proportions of the figure and the ground makes the cover aesthetically striking and dynamic. Human eye used to see classical compositions, in which the figure covers most of the ground. In this design the ground, especially in white resembles the nonexistence, which consistent with the music and the lyrics of the album.

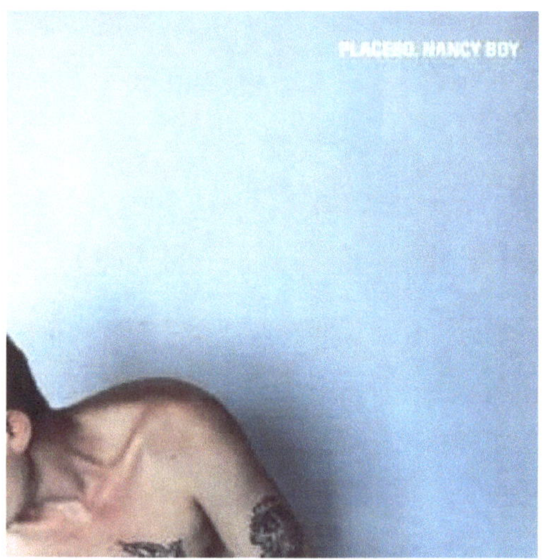

Figure 12. Nancy boy Part 1 of 2 release cover, *Author's collection*

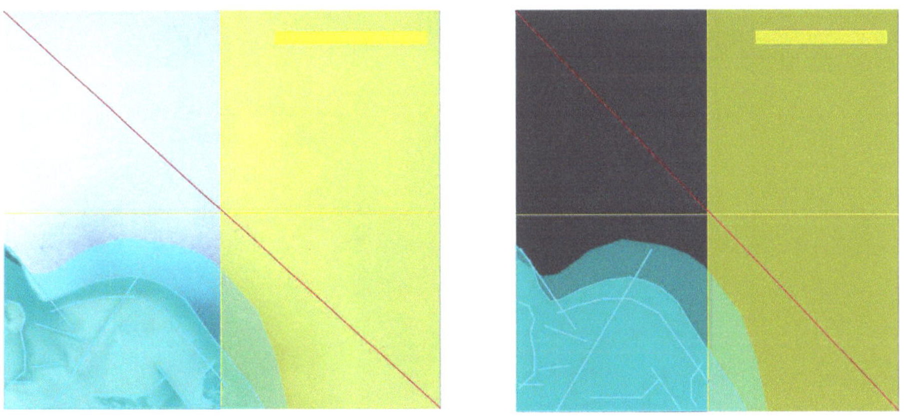

Figure 13. Nancy boy Part 1 of 2 release cover's formal analysis, *by Seker*

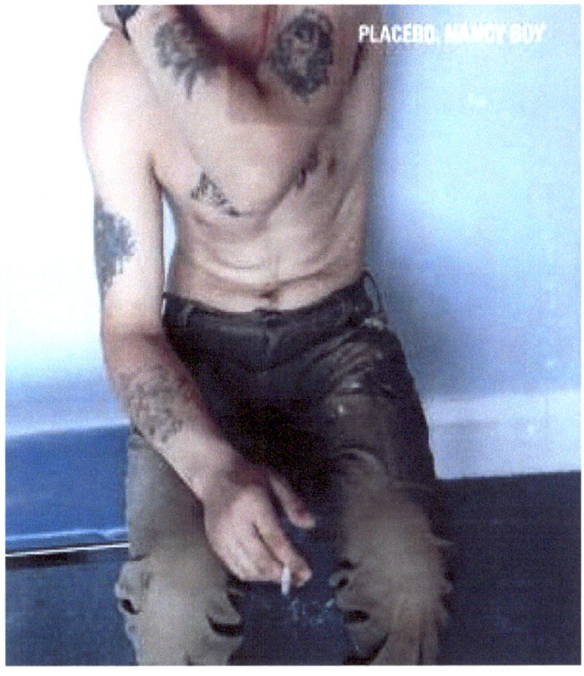

Figure 14. Nancy boy Part 2 of 2 release cover, *Author's collection*

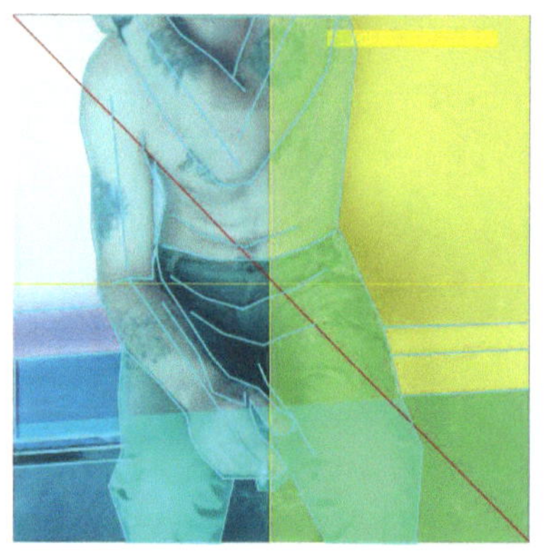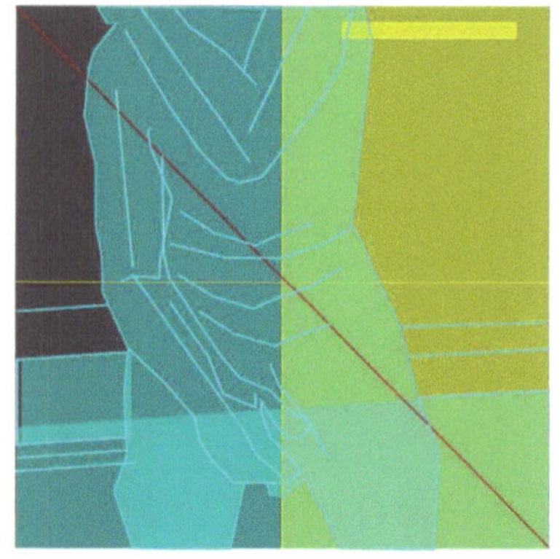

Figure 15. Nancy boy Part 2 of 2 release cover's formal analysis, *by Seker*

On the *Nancy boy Part 2 of 2* cover another extraordinary framing seen: a headless figure from the speaking distance of the viewer standing. The camera focused to the well-built body of the sitting figure, which is topless and covered with tattoos. Human eye used to see the faces as a main medium of communication both in all arts and in real life. The figure placed just next to the center of the surface, sits still but the two arms in different directions bended and skewed intersection of the floor and bench make a huge movement, which makes the whole cover dynamic. This asymmetry helps to maintain every time the general placement, size, and style of typographic elements, which are the name of the band and the release. When examined in detail, it is obviously seen since the *36 degrades* cover the placement getting higher and higher, step by step millimetrically. The down going hand and denim combined with the shades of the ground are balanced by the up going dense lettering and tattoos mostly lay on the upper half of the design surface.

The first single *Bruise Pristine* re-recorded in 1997 and released in two parts as titled like the *Nancy Boy* as *Bruise Pristine Part 1 of 2* and *Bruise*

Pristine Part 2 of 2. It is the last single release from their first studio album. (Thompson, 2010: 159)

The cover set design as the next step of the nude canon and minimalist expression, which based on the *less is more* design idea with neat and clean lines (Ramakers, 2012: 7). Two semi reflective metallic surfaces attached as a semi diagonal corner covered the whole design surface. A newborn seen in the real-life photography naked while breastfeeding on her mother's naked body. The couple cropped diagonally, the camera focused to the baby's face and distorted semi reflection on the metallic surface. The proportion among the figure and the ground are again just the opposite what the human eye used to. The leading actor of this photograph is the metal background not the figure from the proportional perspective. Besides being the first female figure seen on the Placebo release covers, the faceless mother figure seen on the cover is also the next design of the canon called unidentified –but only human- figures. All the parts of the two figures lead the eye to different directions and the axes of these parts intersect with each other as a point of interest in down left. Both the corner with the couple inside placed on left half of the design area and this organization again gives the designer to build the same set up. In this setup the same styled typographic elements in white as a continuing line placed on top right asymmetrically balanced the figure, semi diagonal corner, and distorted shades.

Name given song characterized by its heavy riffs and behind the bridge guitar solo distinguishing for this song can easily be seen on the sharp cold metal walls on the cover photography. The lyrics of the songs are about the pain to be born in this cruel world as a tender soul reflected by the infant, who is in the safe hands of their mother but naked in an odd environment. The changing color scheme into the warmer scale helps to reflect the close relationship, which is still called the neutral color scheme. Neutral as a term means being unbiased, as a color perspective it is about the purity. A color undefined by a definite hue –all kinds of browns- and black & white with all the endless values of greys called generally neutral colors (Harmon, 2013: 9). After examining in detail, it is easily seen all the mentioned neutrals composed the cover design as a mean of color element. The same neutral color scheme applied to the *Bruise pristine part 2 of 2* cover, which is seen on Figure 10. As a cover subject another faceless female figure seen without a baby this time, lying on the floor with a bruise in her arm. On the *Bruise Pristine part 1 of 2* cover the distorted reflection of the figures on the rough metal assumed as a bruise also. She can be presumed as dead or fainted, because of the scattered hair, fallen head and arm. Although longer hair she got than the mother figure on the previous cover, she has similar visual characteristics like white skin, thinness, and dark hair color.

On the floor, tall shadows in tones of grey and greyish browns –neutrals- seen as parallel lines to the figure which all are semi diagonal. A very thin line as a tile part lies in the opposite direction of these shadows, which balanced them asymmetrically with help of the brownish shadow on top left and grey in the middle. On the other hand, the scattered dark hair and figure placed down in the bottom balanced by placing the typographic elements on top closer than ever. The typeface chosen, size, color, and placement attitude, which is consistent made the cover design a signature of Placebo already in the first studio release in a combination with the single releases. Besides the typography used, the composition, proportions, and color schemes consistent in design approach also makes the general cover design an identity of the band Placebo.

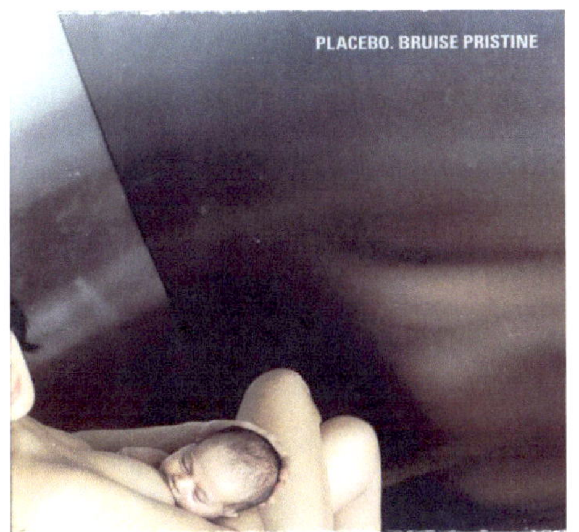
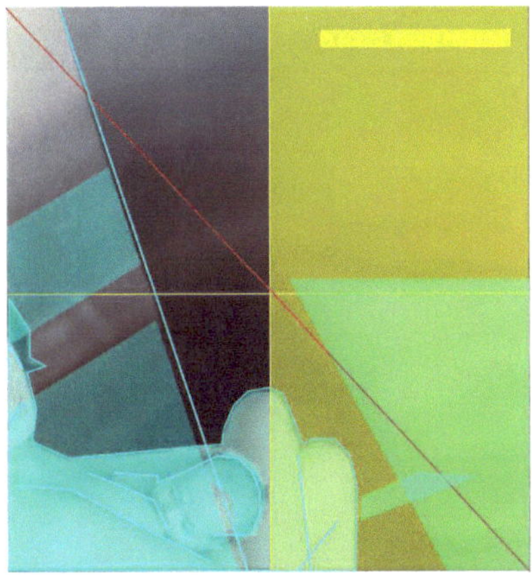

Figure 16. Bruise pristine Part 1 of 2 release cover, Author's collection

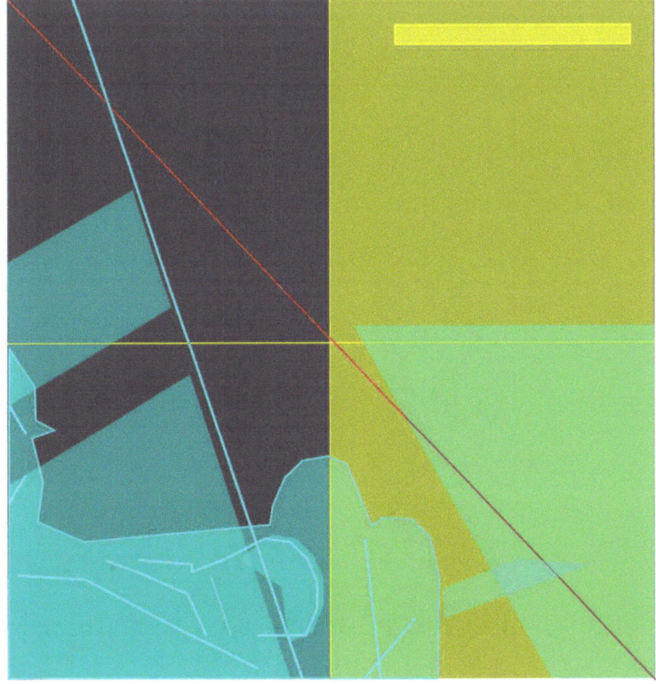

Figure 17. Bruise pristine Part 1 of 2 release cover, *Author's collection*

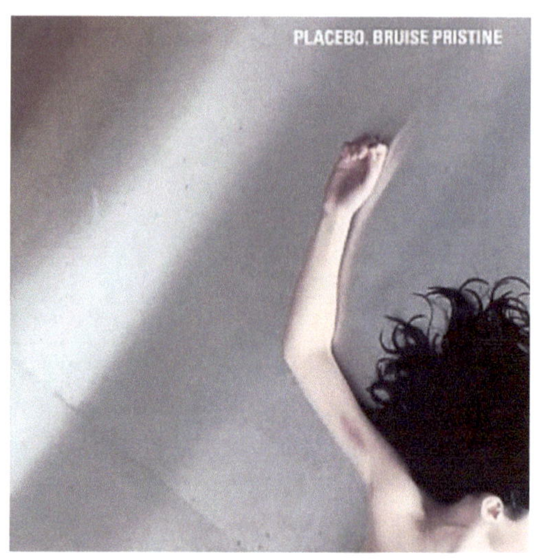

Figure 18. Bruise pristine part 2 of 2 release cover's formal analysis, *by Seker*

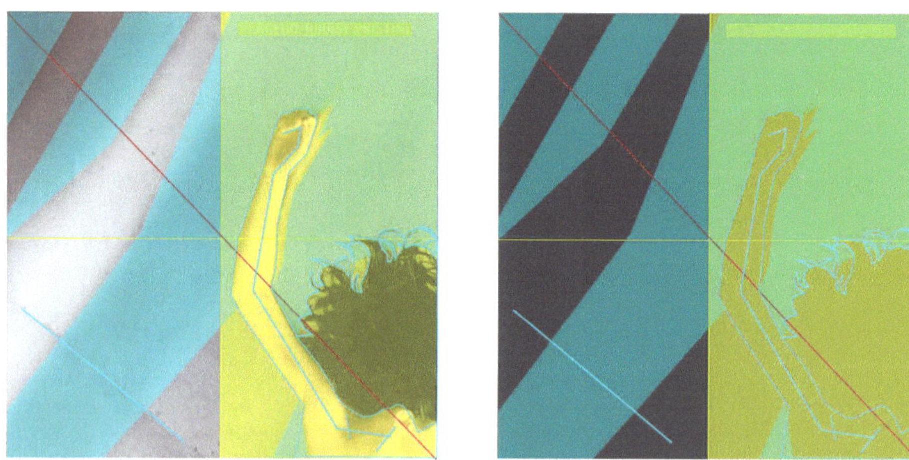

Figure 19. Bruise pristine part 2 of 2 release cover's formal analysis, *by Seker*

Pure morning released in August 1998 as the first single of the band's second studio album *Without you I'm nothing,* although it was a lastminute addition (Geffen, 2020: 82). On the cover the part 1 of 2, a real-life photograph used as a one-piece ground, which covers the whole area, suits the general design attitude. The theme chosen is an outdoor environment within an old concrete empty swimming pool and its concrete tiles within an open garden captured with wild green bushes. Based on the main theme, the photograph was taken in an hour in the very early morning, when it is luminous, neat, and clean with cold colors without any sun.

With the paddle inside the swimming pool and its seaweed covered surface in different dark and light but neutral greens covers the general surface. The rest of the cover filled with neutrals like grey and greyish blues in tint and shades with little touches of ten. An air photo-shooting technic used to capture an extraordinary framing shows the couple lying in the pool and the boy sitting almost at the farthest side still can be seen.

The diagonal main side of the pool placed just above the golden section of the ideal geometry of the golden square of 1:1 (Griffing, 2007: 108). The three parted line in the form of a pool edge turning as an angular axe, lead the eye turning inside the cover and scan the whole cover. The eye traces the puddle ends up with the beginning of the same loop also covers the three figures. The dynamism of the cover design is understandable also besides these diagonals and the textural contrast in between the two substances, which are the bushes and the concrete with the third one: skin – fabric – hair combination, human figure. The dynamic perspectives of all the elements used are asymmetrically balanced with the typography applied by keep the style, size, placement, and color, which is grey but as light as perceived as the lightest element of the cover. Besides the break given to the nude canon and colorless color schemes, the one-image + one-line-one-kind typography cover design attitude continues. Still instead of human figure, the place it / they installed dominates the cover.

Getting deep into the theme is chosen for the cover of the *Pure morning part 2 of 2*. Presumed as the detail of the couple in the pool lying together, are seen on the cover as a group portrait. A Klimtian* like composition seen in this serene and peaceful hug within sleep (Neret, 2005: 74). The proportions of classical portraits left aside, the camera focused on the feeling reflected by the gestures of body and parts instead of identities. This extraordinary framing has extraordinary proportions, directions and grift structure created by the parts caused dynamism fallows a continuing loop again and again. Cold colors dominated color scheme is still low saturated. Both the textures of the concrete ground with seaweed residues on it and the sweatshirt emphasize the perfect pure skins of the two. By tracing it another loop occurs with help of the arms and hands wrapped around each other. And finally, these loops fixed with the help of three black spots in a triangular relation with each other, the hair of the boy, the blouse, and the armbands of the girl. With help of the typographical canon, both the horizontal and vertical lines of the arms repeated and stopped by the lettering, in which the eye has just begin to read.

The fourth single release from the album was *You don't care about us* at the end of the September 1998 (Larkin, 2011: 2000). The release has two parts as recently seen in all the band's single releases. *The part 1 of 2* consists of three songs, first the name given, then the legendary *20th Century Boy* song of the legendary band *T. Rex* and finally an instrumental Placebo piece titled *Ion* (Whitt & Perlich, (Eds.) 2014: 52).

T. Rex was a legendary English rock band from late 1960s to late 1970s. With the *Tyrannosaurus Rex* era before 1970, it was a very productive decade with 12 studio albums they made. Psychedelic folk music they are making turned into electric rock by the leadings of the former member *Marc*

Bolan. While acoustic instrumentation with psychedelic elements turned into glam rock with all its glittering outrageous costumes, makeup and wide range musical styles from cabaret, science fiction to art rock, T. Rex became a significant band interrupted by a sad incident. The 29-year-old member Bolan died in a car crash in 1977 while sitting in the passenger seat near the driver, who was his very loving *Gloria Jones.* As an implication to this causeless car accident a greyish blue car standing on a side seen on the cover of the release in an undefined setup but on plain sand with a little blue sea in the back under a quite cloudless blue sky. (Henderson, 2001: 91; Stanton, 2003: 287)

In front of the angled giant car two boys seen cowered facing to each other but looking in other directions as if they are just got off from it. The different orientation and shapes of the body parts and the car makes the composition dynamic in front of a contrastingly calm background. The two separate planes balance each other in a neutral color scheme dominated by neutral blues chosen for the whole set. Besides these blues, different tones of creamy greys, neutral greens, black and white used with in a combination.

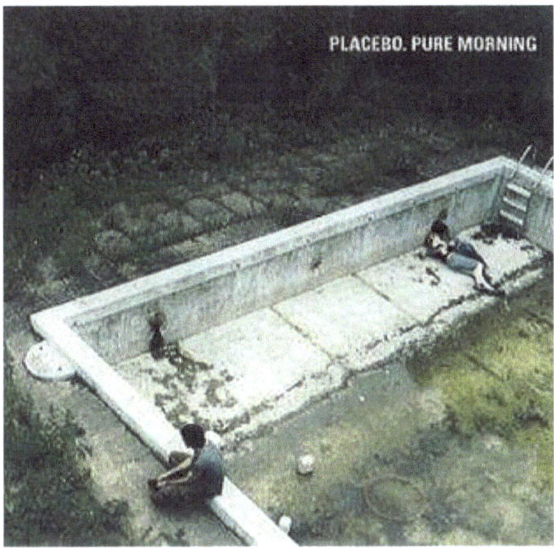

Figure 20. Pure morning part 1 of 2 release cover, *Author's collection*

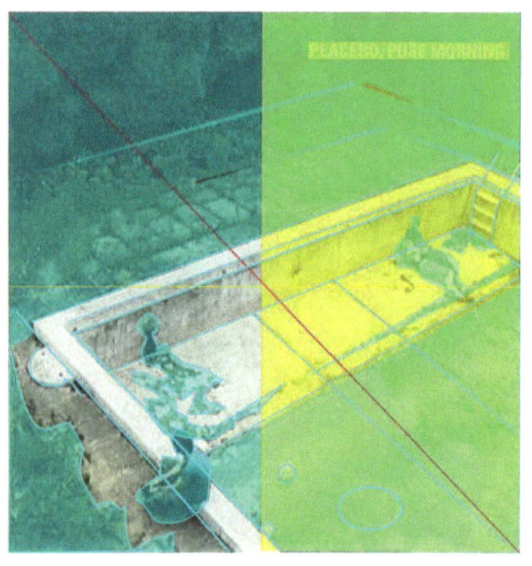
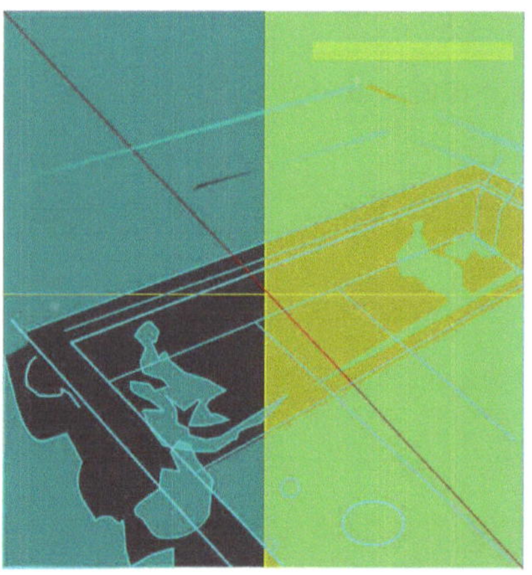

Figure 21. Pure morning part 1 of 2 release cover's formal analysis, *by Seker*

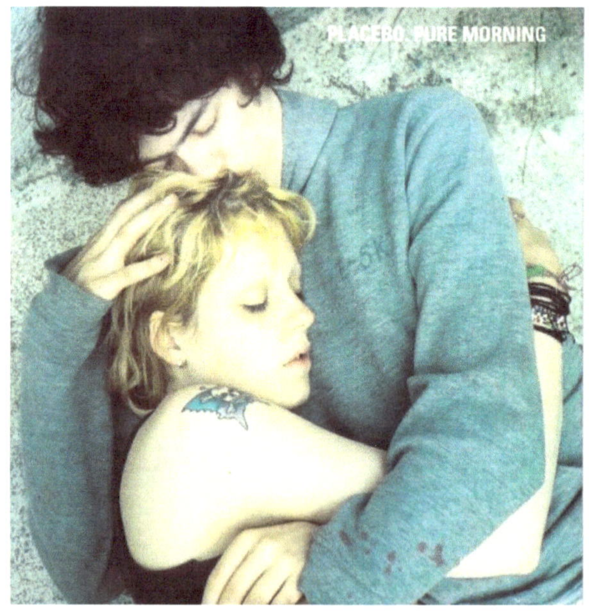

Figure 22. Pure morning part 2 of 2 release cover, *Author's collection*

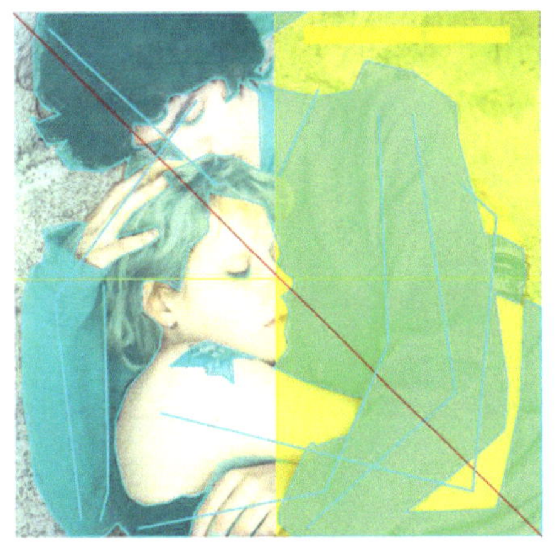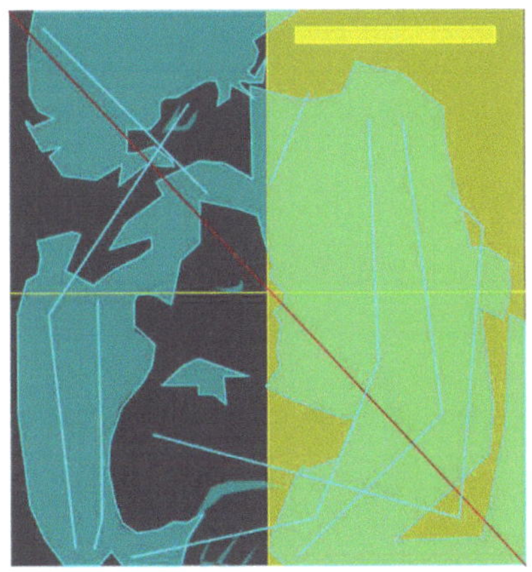

Figure 23. Pure morning part 2 of 2 release cover's formal analysis, *by Seker*

The consistently designed typographic elements for writing the name of the band and the album placed in the similar location closer to the top in same size: as small as they can still be red with the help of the most light tone, which is white. Another version of the same incident seen on the cover of the *You don't care about us part 2 of 2* again in a real-life photograph, which reflects the scene with bare eyes in real life. Before or after the accident scene from far seen on the photograph. The car seen on its tires with doors wide open in the middle of a semi-sandy shore with the boys standing on the left, faced to each other but their heads down. The unusual proportions of the composition took the attention of the viewer by making the scene vogue and secondary besides the grains of the giant sand covers more than the third. The rest filled with the story comprised with the car, boys, the sea, and the sky. The groups placed diagonally in the flattened but wide rectangular area from left bottom to right top evenly by placing the car in the middle and as a final touch the dark red flying sweater asymmetrically balanced the typographic elements, which are relatively as the wider item after the sea, the sky and the sandy beach.

While the design of the second version suits the first, the two also are reflecting the subject themes of the two songs on unrequited love, friendship and same sex relations, which are *You don't care about us* and *Pure morning*. While deep sadness in these songs reflects itself by the neutral color scheme, which perceived as cold and senseless, the emptiness of the beach prevents the eye to move. The viewer automatically stares to the horizon and this concluded in relaxation but also alienation and estrangement, which are the subjects of the whole release set, so accepted as reflecting the release as visually on sleeves.

The second studio album *Without you I'm nothing* labeled as alternative rock released in October 1998 after the two single releases from its track listing (Whitburn, 1999: 138). Like the previous sleeve set subjected two boys facing each other but looking down without any conversation the cover photograph used subjected two girls facing each other but looking down without any conversation. The girls are very much looking each other as face, body, outfit, and hair styles. The only exception is the hair color, which breaks down the mirror effect with the help of the slightly changing angles and arms tied. The over bright sun shines coming from the window curtain painted the room into a dark yellow. The sunlight increased the depth effect in the symmetrical composition, which has a pivotal point in the middle and make the stability dynamic without any movement (Landa, 2014: 147). The asymmetries caused by opposite positioning of the hands and postures balanced only by the classical typography used with all its features. When examining in detail no extraordinary proportions used, because the mirror effect in the middle is fair enough to create the unexpectedly uncommon.

The dramatically changing color scheme caused by sunlight a quality of nature but not a neutral color, but just the opposite: it is the one of the three primaries, which are red, blue, and yellow (Sherin, 2013: 73). They are used as they are in a row on the previous sleeves as one by one as the dominating color on different sleeves. The sunlight covers all the room turned the color scheme into a monochromatic color scheme consist the tint and shades until it became pitch black. Pitch black and white is the maximums of the monochromatic scheme, which do not harm but ensures and enriches it.

All songs with their sad stories represented by this stable, monotonous, and still photograph. Lack of motion effect, inexpressive faces and down-looking thinking mood of the figures are the indicators of these unhappy ending stories. Like the photography as a creative technique, nudes and definite color modes continuing from the beginning, there is also another cannon seen in the form of apathetic or crying facial expressions on the sleeve art of the band just in the production of their second studio album, but with many single releases they've already made.

An outdoor photograph used as a subject for the sleeve of *Every you and every me part1 of 2* single release dated January 1999 as the third from the second studio release (www.discogs.com). A giant white caravan seen under a blue summer sky among wild lilac summer flowers, which generally used as a house by the libertarians, outsiders or people prefer to live in nature. The caravan divided the design area into two halves vertically, which are full of sky and full of bushes. The caravan seen from ¾ of rear and its perspective is not emphasized but slightly perceived as an asymmetry (Pentak & Lauer, 2016: 274). This asymmetry balanced by a naked figure in the door, two dark windows, and a giant dark tree on right by a giant bush with the biggest lilac flowers on it on the left side. Nudity cannon can be traced not easily but if examined in detail the nearly as white as the caravan figure can be seen. The white typography placed on top right also helped to this setup in same style, size, and approach.

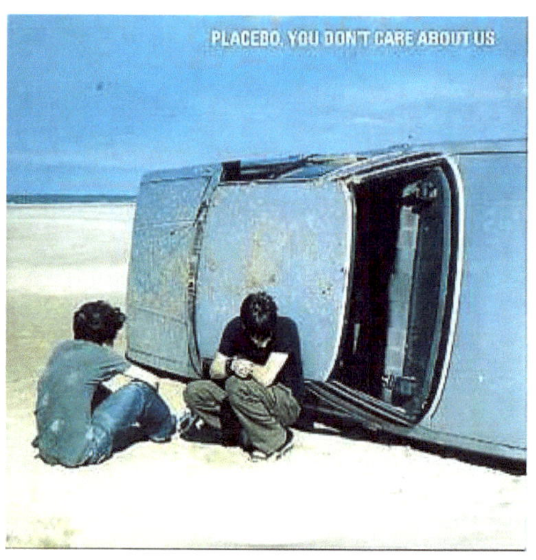

Figure 24. You don't care about us release cover, *Author's collection*

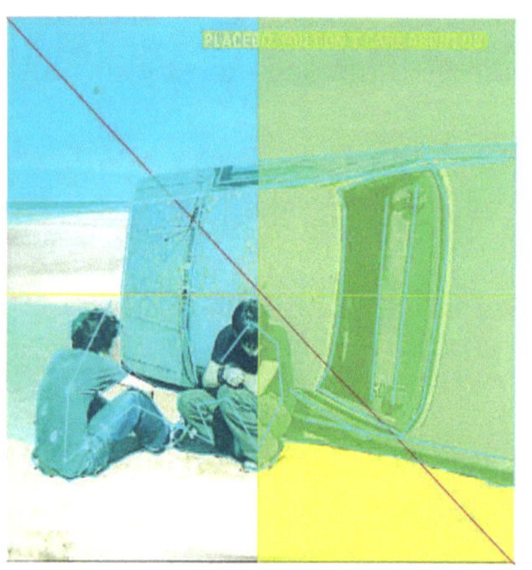

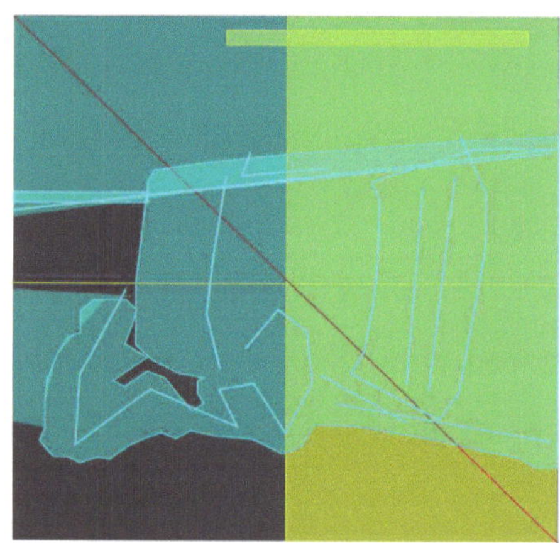

Figure 25. You don't care about us release cover's formal analysis, *by Seker*

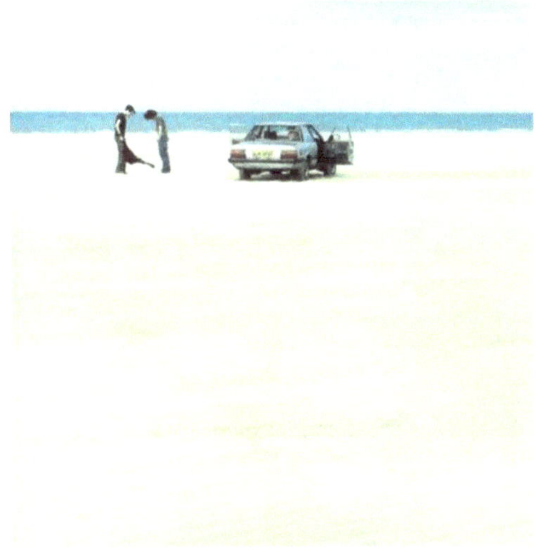

Figure 26. You don't care about us part 2 of 2 release cover, *Author's collection*

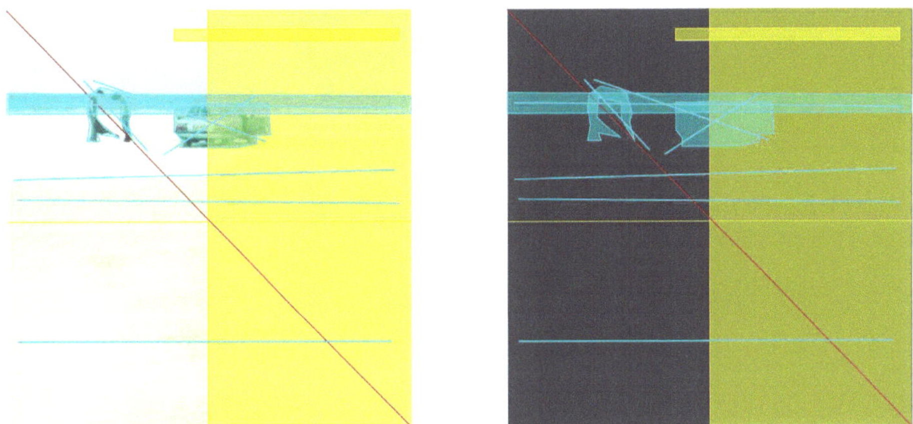

Figure 27. You don't care about us part 2 of 2 release cover's formal analysis, *by Seker*

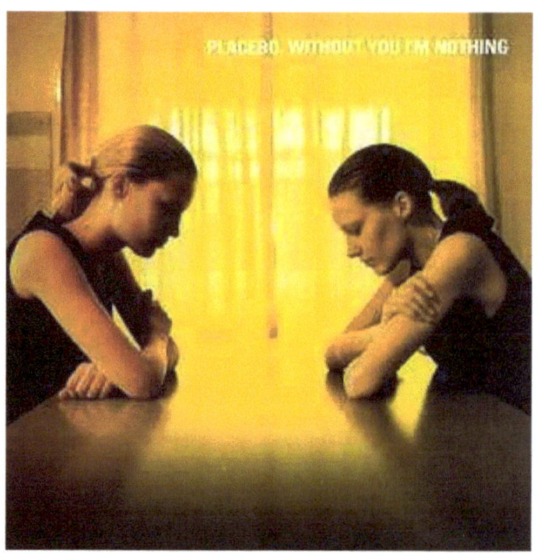

Figure 28. Without you I'm nothing release cover, *Author's collection*

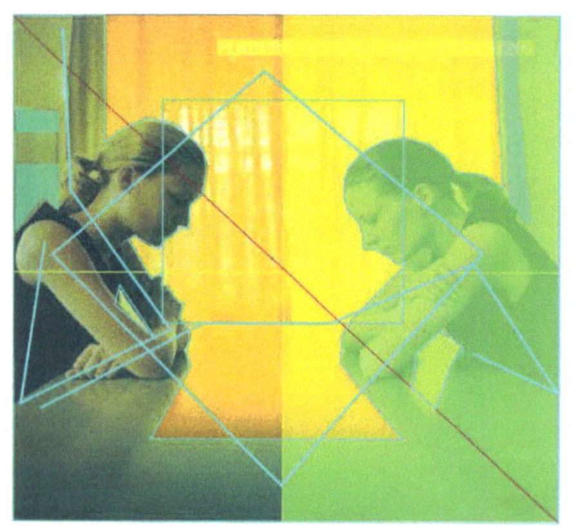 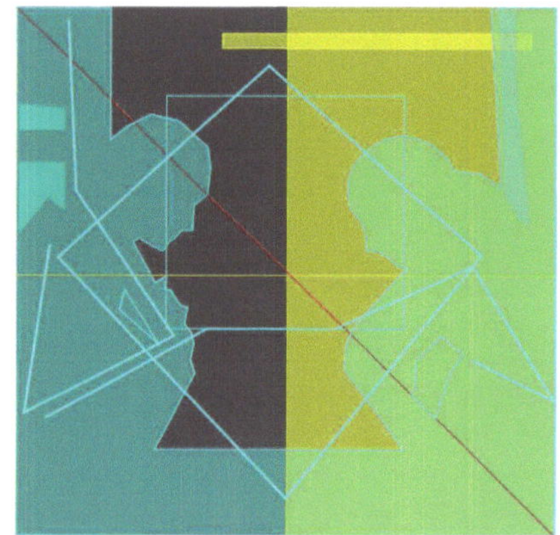

Figure 29. Without you I'm nothing release cover's formal analysis, *by*

Seker

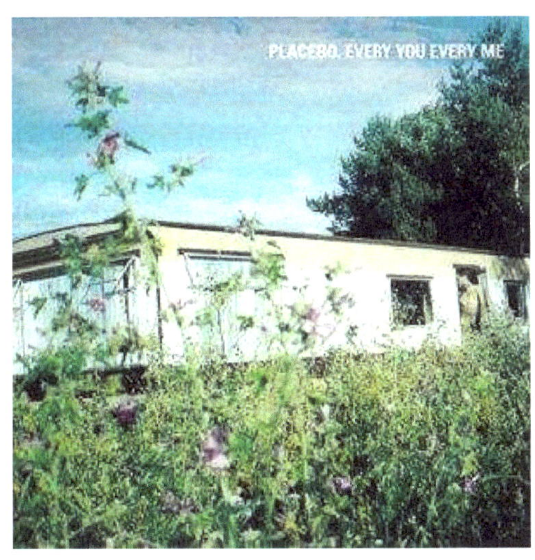

Figure 30. Every you every me part 1 of 2 release cover, *Author's collection*

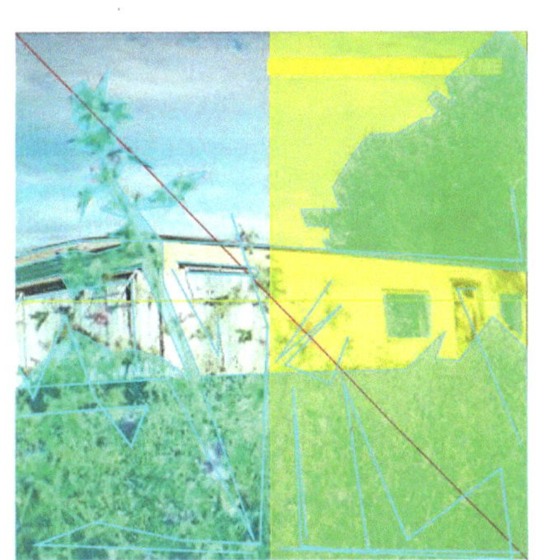 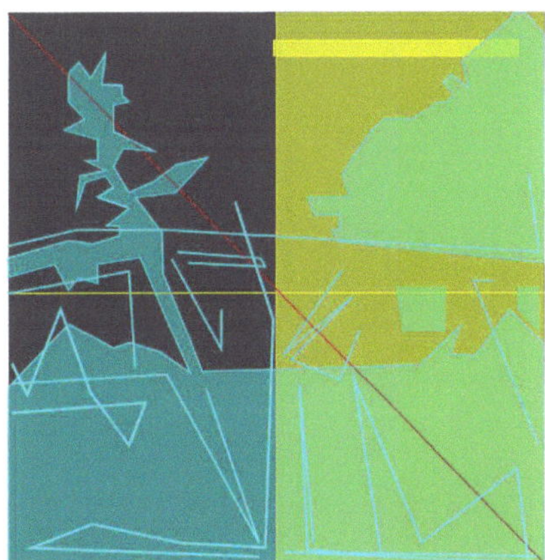

Figure 31. Every you every me part 1 of 2 release cover's formal analysis, *by Seker*

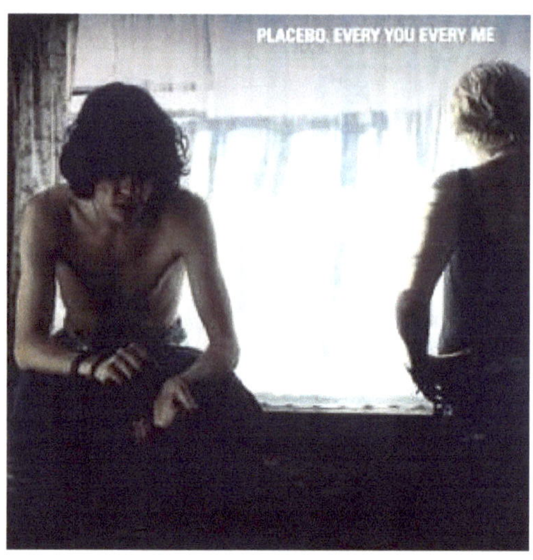

Figure 32. Every you every me part 2 of 2 release cover, *Author's collection*

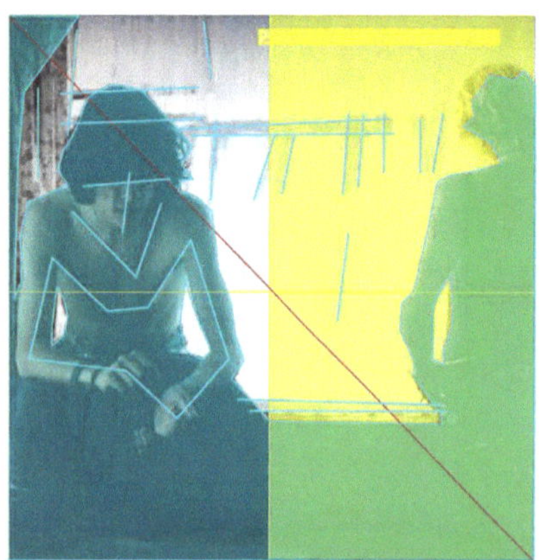

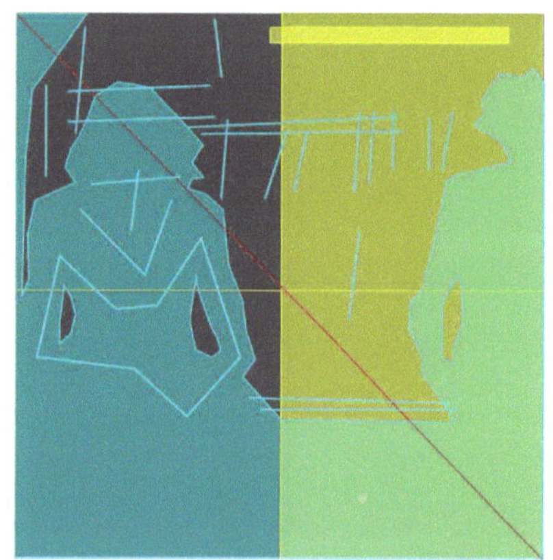

Figure 33. Every you every me part 2 of 2 release cover's formal analysis, *by Seker*

The natural color scheme as the previous two single releases is consistent and as a design attitude it is called the continuity, which helped the viewer to perceive these products are parts of a whole set and they are unite (Wong, 1972: 53). Although blue sky covers less than 1/3 of the cover, it is the most enchanting color of the design. The rest subordinate this by their natural harmony. Any artificial coloring disrupts the viewer, only white, which adds freshness. Although it is artificially created for the caravan and the lettering, it is not a color, but paint only. White is the color of light, which is the sum of the whole light beams. When it is not absorbed by the surface, it reflected to the eye as a whole and human eye perceived it as white. If all the beams absorbed the surface and nothing reflected, there would be any light of beams, nothing equals black. If only red-light beams were reflected to the eye and the rest absorbed by the apple, it is seen as red. So finally, with the help of all the almost white clouds and the dancing light all over the wild bushes the sleeve shimmers like the caravan, letters, and the skin of the figure harmfully. (Feisner, 2006: 23)

For the *Every you and every me part 2 of 2* single release, an indoor photograph used, which is thematically suits to the studio album the single release belongs to. A frame looking directly to the window from which the light comes through the curtains closed into a dark room. The symmetrical centered composition balanced by two figures in both sides, like the bold and brunette figures sitting at the table. In this design the symmetry both broken down and balanced at the same time with the postures of the figures: one female - one male, one standing – one sitting, one seen from front, one from back, and finally again one blond – one brunette with similar hair styles, which are free. The vertically half figure on the right built a team with the typographic elements on top of her as the right side of the equilibrium. The topless boy sitting in front of the darker curtain with the patterns seen with both hands with the white lines towards hic side asymmetrically balanced the rest. The indoor photography dazzled with the bright light coming from the window. This dazzling turned the colors into neutrals in different tints and shades of low saturation (Rhyne, 2016: 3-14). The objects and figures in front of a light source perceived as shades. This is the cause the semi shady silhouettes in front of the bar. The white skin of the boy presumed as seen at the door of the caravan on the previous sleeve, turned into a darker tone. On the other hand, the window itself, curtains, some skin parts, and blonde hair became brighter with the help of direct light on them. This tint – shade setup makes the scene dramatic. Because the lack of or reduced number of the middle tones the contrast of the photography increased as amount. Almost black & white perceived sleeve's lettering suits the color scheme used. The more contrast, the more negative feelings and emotions represented, like in the lyrics of the name given single (Finger, Zaidel, Boller & Bogousslavsky (Eds.), 2013: 198).

After the fourth single release in August 1999 with the famous British cult musician of the 20th century David Bowie (Gulla, 2006: 199), the fifth and final single released in the same year in November was *Burger Queen Français* (www.discogs.com). While Pacebo - Bowie single release was a live performance in New York and its sleeve based on a black & white New York cityscape, which creates a gap in Placebo sleeve art canon, so left out of the selection analyzed in this book, on the other hand *Burger Queen Français'* sleeve design is the first application of a new set of design approach, which will be obvious after the *Black Market Music* set. The time dimension added to the sleeve art in the form of a special photography technique created by juxtaposing many angles, which perceived as a moving image with the help of blurred and / or sharp layers seen on the same image.

Like on many previous and upcoming sleeves the gender and gender combinations of the figures photographed are various, so gender bended.

Whether the song is about the story of a "he" the sleeve art could be a "she" looks feminine or not. On a pitch-black ground, a blond female figure seen as portrait with apathetic look in her face under the effect of saying no by shaking her head into two sides. Dressing as a pitch-black dress without sleeves makes the costume out of main theme according to one of the visual perception rules, which is *figure-ground.* In this rule it is said that the similar visual qualifications perceived as a whole and the human eye tent to presume it either figure or ground for a better perception by comparing the visual in real environment it lives in (Ramirez, 2013: 234). Pitch black dress and the background perceived as a whole background because they are black, they perceived in deep besides the lighter tones of blond hair and white skin. The eye immediately focuses on the white skin and the moving effect on the face, so they both dominating the sleeve. The symmetrical composition of a female portrait became something dynamic, live and moving. The typographic signature of the band and the single's name on top right with its solitude -there is nothing to balance this placement this time- suits very much to the movement created horizontally. No coloring and high contrast among the figure and the ground make the scene dramatic and serious like the theme of the single.

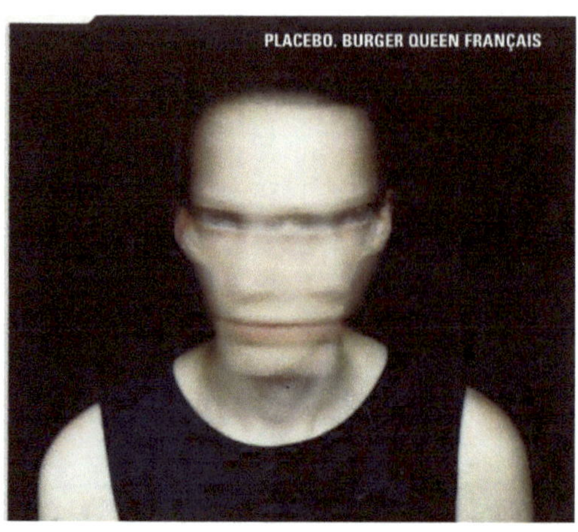

Figure 34. Burger queen français release cover, *Author's collection*

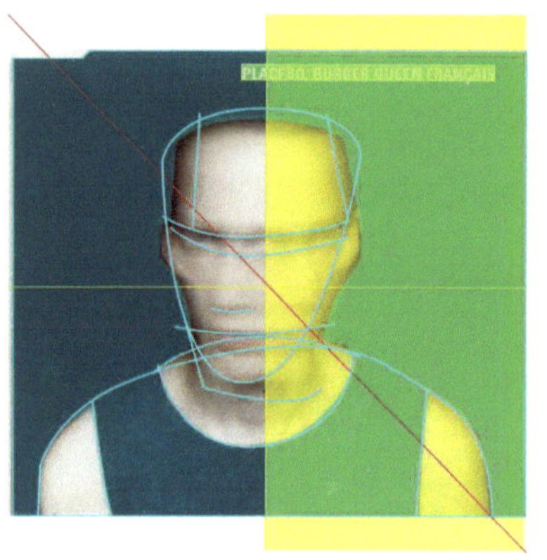

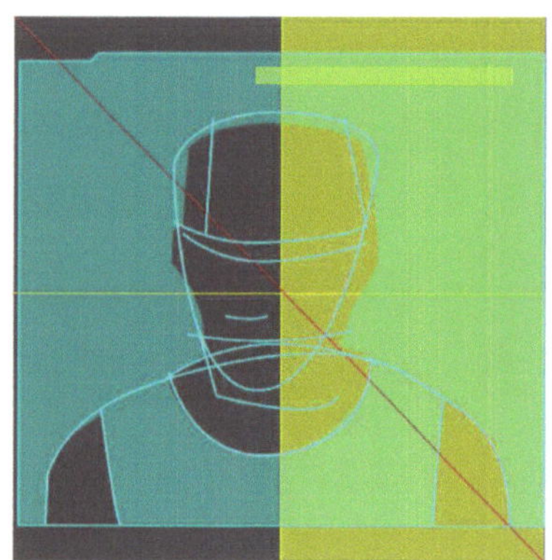

Figure 35. Burger queen français release cover's formal analysis, *by Seker*

The third studio album of the band, *Black market music* introduced with the *Taste in men* as the 12th single release in the July 2000: while the album labeled as alternative rock the single release labeled electronic rock by fusing the two musical styles like dub mix made by Adrian Sherwood, who is an English record producer (www.allmusic.com). Although musically consistent the sleeve design attitude looks different at first sight. While the human figure-oriented photography replaced by object-oriented, the naturalistic photographic style replaced by a digitally effect applied ones. Metal looks like gold or brass chosen as a thematic medium in a combination with neutrals. With the ongoing studio releases, it will be obviously seen that this design attitude only seen in the *Black market music* and its related products.

The second track *Theme from funky reverend* titled instrumental composition in funk music, which consist of rhythm and blues, soul, jazz in a danceable form. The various sized and styled metal spoons spread on surface randomly are meaningful with the help of the info. The limited number of colors used prevent the chaos can be caused by these variables and put the artwork in design and unite it with the album itself. The spoons turned into brass instruments with the help of this coloring, but the shiny bright perfection of brass reduced by high levels of tonal contrasts. Tonal contrasts made by reducing the number of the millions of tones into countable ones, which can be traced by definite areas. This increases the size of the areas of the definite tones, both the darkest and the brightest perceived as black and white by human eye easily. The contrasting effect among tones, which reflects the fusion in between the musical styles suit the contrasting background and the coloring chosen for the typography. Coloring is the term used, because the two are surface qualifications but not colors: black & white, the best options both being visible, harmonious, and subordinating to the leading characters: the spoons.

The track list of the *Taste in men part 2 of 2* release consist besides two versions of the name given song a covered version of the 1980 dated Robert Palmer song titled *Johnny and Mary* (Binnie, 2018: 174). Palmer was a world-wide known English rock musician, who combines soul, jazz, pop, rock, reggae and blues very well. Three years before Palmer died as age 54 unexpectedly, the band had released the single by stating that they found the song very sad and touching (http://traductionsetparoles.over-blog.com). This could be the cause of the vintage or classical silver spoons photograph used on the sleeve design with lesser amounts of visual effects, unlike the plain spoons on the sleeve art of Part 1 of 2, which applied visual effects highly. On black plain surface the spoons organized on horizontal-vertical axes, which suits to the classic theme of the unhappy love song. With the help of the dark background, reduced amount of contrasting and coloring, the metallic texture dominated. The styles of the spoons became visible and dominating the cover with their tonal variety both suits the white typography, black background, and the *Part 1 of 2* sleeve's color scheme, which is neutral.

The typography used is the same as ever as style and placement, but larger in size to be seen easily among all the spoons and their long-thin but curvy shapes. Also, the horizontal-vertical arrangement made for a calmer design, because of the unstable thicknesses of the handles of the spoons. Being bare and all alone, the spoons are fallowing the nude canon with their monochrome coloring and texture like human skin. Besides these qualifications their curvy shapes and regular geometric structure can be related to the basic geometry forms the human body. Being on plain surfaces generally suits to the whole set of sleeve art even in the form of blue sky or a plain creamy white wall.

The same year's second release from the *Black music market* album titled as *Slave to wage* is presents another option, which has the same design concept applied by other objects: coins, which is the visible subject of the single (www.amazon.es). Ancient coins from different eras and civilizations photographed first according to an open composition, which creates the effect that a detail seen from the big picture. While the size and shape variety chosen enriches the visual, the square holes on some of the coins create a connotation with the rest of the cover. On the other hand, the size, direction, and location contrasts on plain white background create a dynamic effect, which makes the surface interesting and unusual, so attractive.

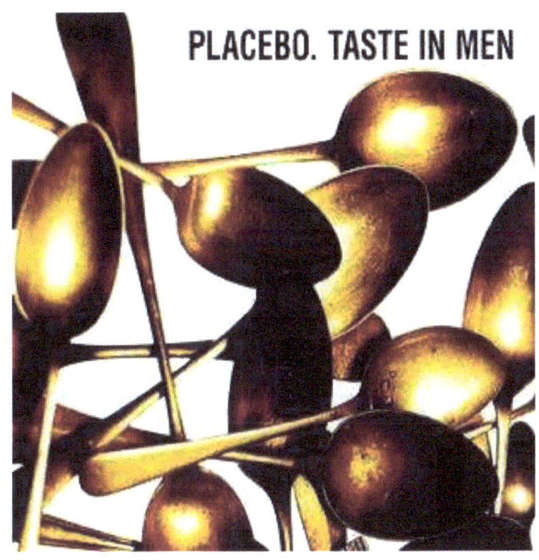

Figure 36. Taste in men part 1 of 2 release cover, *Author's collection*

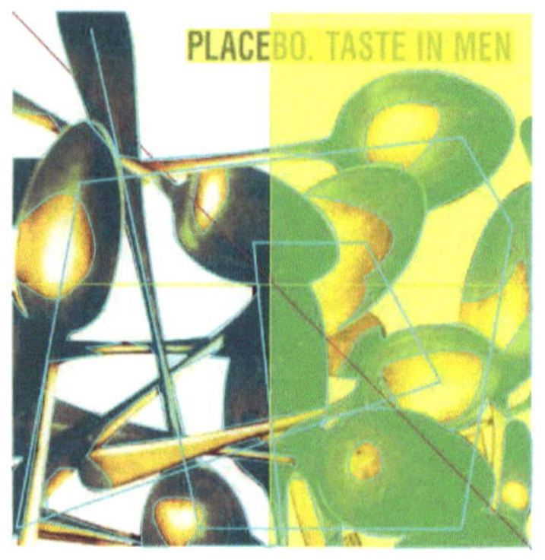

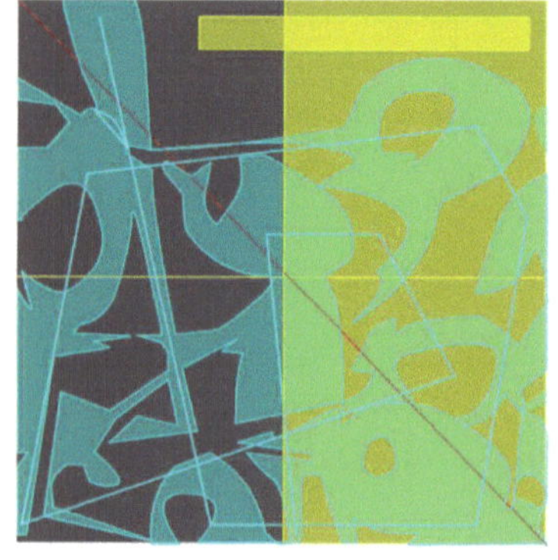

Figure 37. Taste in men part 1 of 2 release cover's formal analysis, *by Seker*

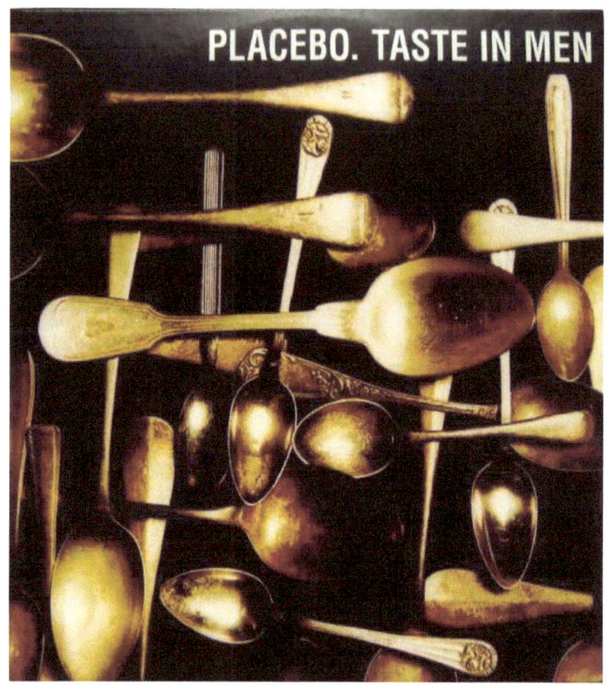

Figure 38. Taste in men part 2 of 2 release cover, *Author's collection*

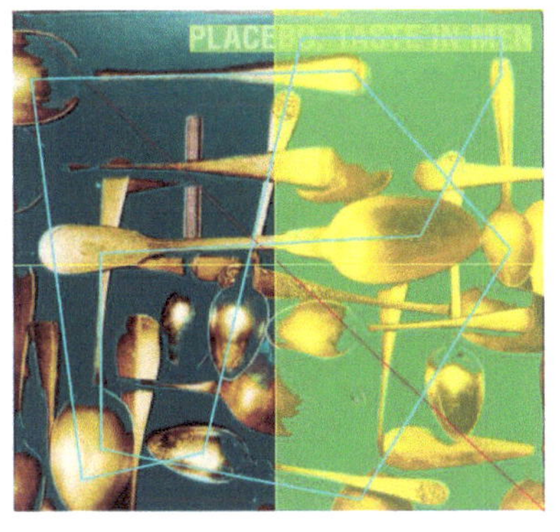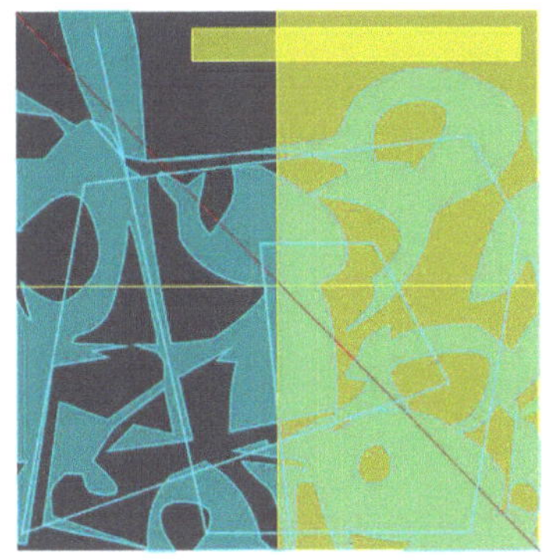

Figure 39. Taste in men part 2 of 2 release cover's formal analysis, *by Seker*

The old and thorn surface of the coins colored by the neutral color scheme, which is not exact but very similar to the previous covers, *Taste in man*. With the help of the shades and white plain background, which are just the opposite, helps the coins to be the most dominating aspect of the surface. The irregular space organized to base the typographic elements, which are the names of the release and the band. The size contrasts among the coins reflected to the typographic element groups. This approach used for the first time supports the dynamism but breaks the ongoing cannon to create a new sleeve art style.

Like the previous single releases, in this release 1978 dated song *Holocaust* of the band Big Star covered by Placebo. Big star was an American rock band from Memphis, Tenessee formed in 1971 by Chris Bell with Alex Chilton, Jody Stephens, and Andy Hummel. Immediately after the first studio album titled *#1 Record* failed to achieve commercial success Bell left the band to pursue his own solo career. In 1978 when he was death after a rehearsal in a car accident, he was suffering from depression, alcohol, and drug problems. After the death of Bell, the second break up came from Hummel, who left the band to go to university for a degree in literature. *Holocaust* was a song from the third album of the band, in which only two constant members were struggle for. (Hoskyns, 2003: 310)

Slave to wage part 2 of 2 was released afterwards consist only the titling single plus remixed version and the Chilton song *Holocaust,* who always cited by his seminal influence on rock musicians. Chilton in his 44 years of music career was a singer – songwriter, guitarist, record producer and the lead singer of the bands the Box Tops and the Big Star (Dimery & Rodeia, 2020: 37). It was a song about the World War II genocide of the European Jews, which afterwards shocks the rest of the world in pain and anger (Darman (Ed.), 2013: 10).

Like the *Taste in men* pair, *Slave to wage part 2 of 2* created an alternative composition made by using the same elements but in different relations. Another detail chosen from the big picture, same coloring and contrasting effects applied, and placed on a pitch-black background. Like the white plain ground, black is just the opposite of every color / value and has similar function as contrasting with the rest to make them more visible and attractive.

The diagonal asymmetrical composition, which created by the figure-ground relations has left the traditional place for typographic elements. With size differences the two placed as two rows, aligned from left in white to become the most contrasting value to be seen and red. No bright colors used like red or yellow to manage the dark mood the sleeve art will transfer. Being just the opposite of the white ground, the black background let the coins to be perceived as the closest objects and let the eye of the viewer to fallow the detailed drawings and letters on them, which are fallowing organic form cannon. Whereas the white background as being the lightest and the brightest of the surface perceived as if it is before or at least in the same level of the coins, which let the coins perceived as they are not the leading but helping roles of the sleeve art. The white shines like a bright light comparing with the rest of the sleeve, but the black types on white is the most contrasting combination like in the basic legibility systematic: black writings on white paper.

While the circles of the coins in different sizes but in same proportions repeating creates a harmonious rhythm and a repetition, the three squares holed coins creates another with the help of the square shaped sleeve itself. These rhythm and repetition with the help of the type create a loop, which leads the eye of the viewer on the whole sleeve and scan it again and again (Murphy, 2009: 217). Like the changing sizes of the coins, the changing sizes of the types support and make the design much more dynamic.

Labeled as alternative rock, *Black market music* was the third studio album released in October 2000 both before and after two single releases. On the sleeve a dark, mono chrome photograph of a mechanism from inside a barrel organ / a music box used (Weiss-Stauffacher, 1976: 13). A very close detail chosen, which has been cut in half, saturated lowly and contrasting highly. The general color scheme for this album and related single releases explained by Molko himself in his interview for Vice that it is a quite monochrome album for him, which is a very deep wood color with stripes of gunmetal grey, when he pictures it (https://www.vice.com).

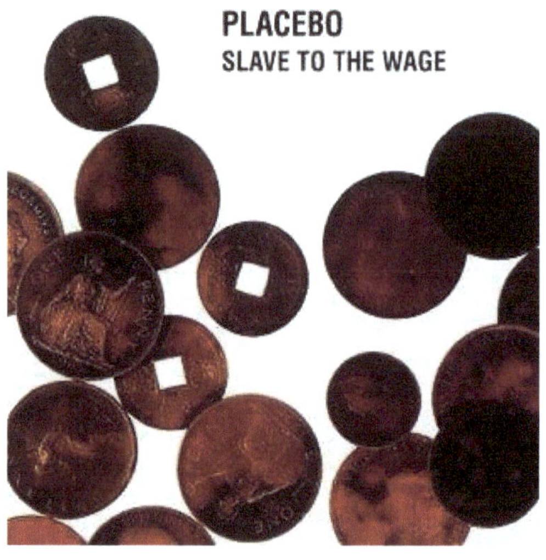

Figure 40. Slave to wage part 1 of 2 release cover, *Author's collection*

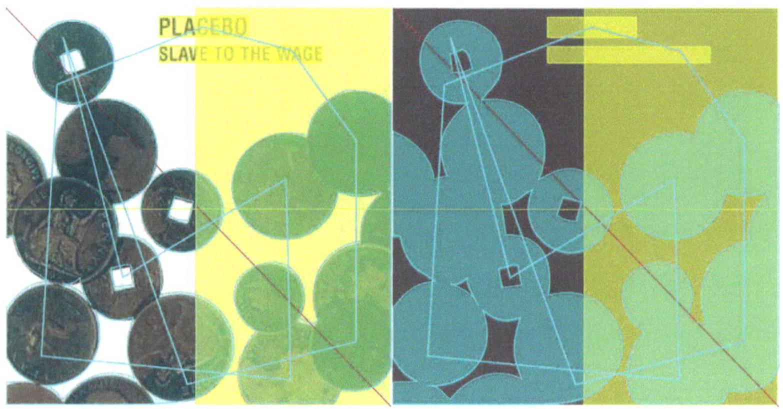

Figure 41. Slave to wage part 1 of 2 release cover's formal analysis, *by Seker*

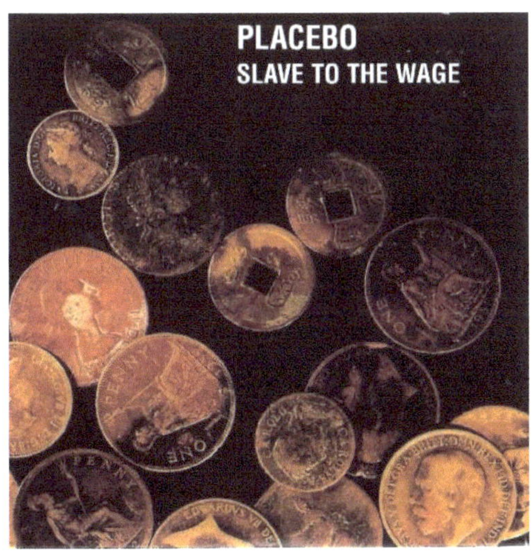

Figure 42. Slave to wage part 2 of 2 release cover, *Author's collection*

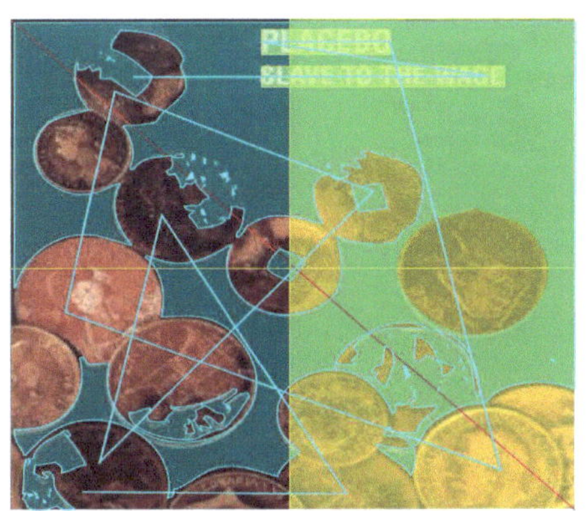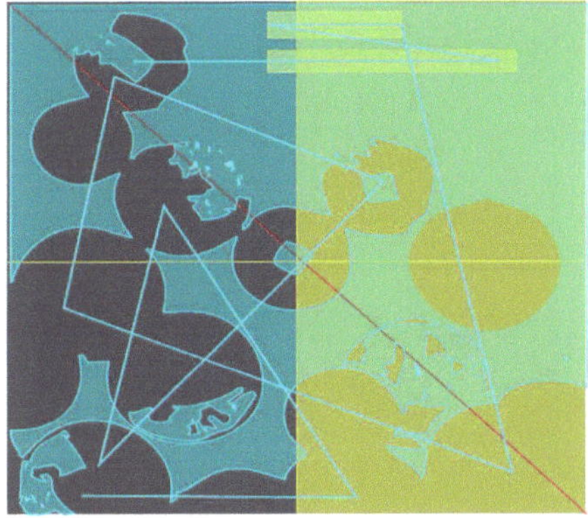

Figure 43. Slave to wage part 2 of 2 release cover's formal analysis, *by Seker*

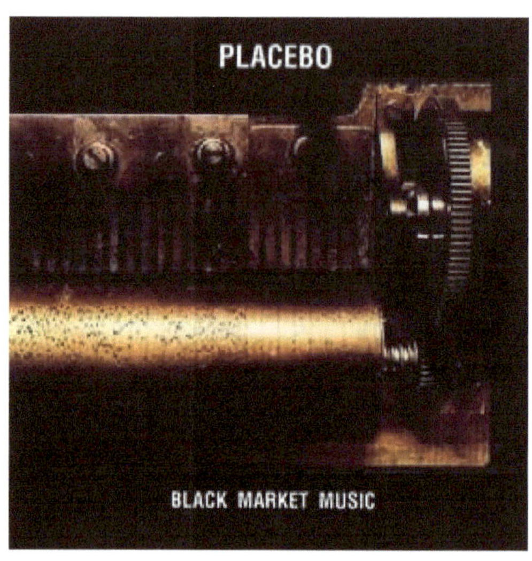

Figure 44. Black market music album cover, *Author's collection*

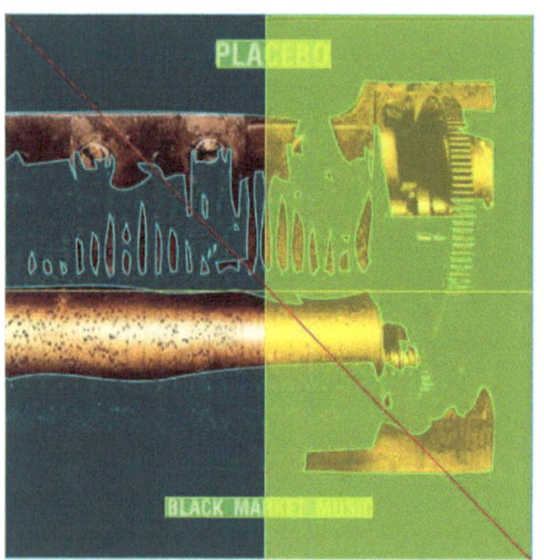
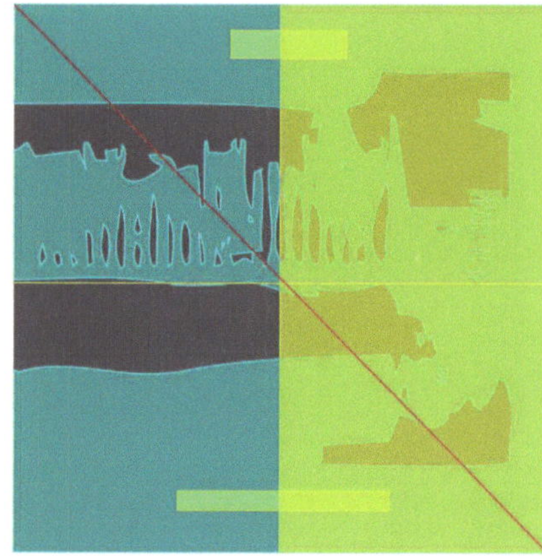

Figure 45. Black market music album cover's formal analysis, *by Seker*

The detail of the metallic mechanism placed as big as it can be from the left side into the surface. This placement formed an asymmetrical dynamism among the cylinder, wheel, and the comb, which again balanced by the same parts. The similar proportion, size and location of the comb and the cylinder have been distracted by the thin deep sharpness of the wheel. The concave characteristic of the mechanism from upper part used to highlight the name of the band, which separated from the album name as size and location. Contrarily to the sleeve art cannon, which used organic forms and materials mainly, a very sharp, solid, and masculine object used to reflect the music inside, accepted by the authorities as the hardest. Besides regular geometric forms and metallic materials, the textural elements consist of regular lines and dots are making the image highly inorganic and rigid with evenly repeating elements.

The pitch-black background is another additional element leads the sleeve art into a darker mood, although it suits to the imagery used. The most contrasting tone, which is white, used to write the typographic elements. The same typeface used in different sizes and locations to indicate the two are different: the name of the band and the name of the album. While the name of the band placed on top in a little bit bigger size than the name of the album on bottom, both aligned from the center, which helps the cover to become a little more stable and heavier. All vertical alignments are made to give some space for legibility both from top and from bottom.

Special k released as the third single from the *Black market music* album in March 2001, which with all its preparations made during 2000 within the scope of the sleeve art made for the whole set of the third studio album (www.amazon.com). For the sleeve art apples within real perspective chosen on a plain ground, which is an indication of turning back to the organic forms, but only forms not the material yet.

A brighter version consists of golden apples suits to the two previous single releases on pure white ground. While apple is a diva among all metaphors in art and in history, golden / gold like apples means multiplying the effect with a precious game changing for the whole world (Harter, 2006: 3).

The leftover apples photographed like groups of people with its general characteristics but special uniqueness' in every detail. Besides the similarities in size and shape, every apple has its own unique form and form-dependent unique direction and stem. All these similar uniqueness' with the help of grouping of the apples and perspective applied makes the photograph highly dynamic unity. Being metallic makes an everyday object something unusual but attractive with all its perfect shine but darker in wood color.

Among millions of tones on every apple shinning the lightest is white like the ground and the darkest is the black used to write the name of the band and the album, which supports the mono chromatic color scheme. The two letter groups placed on same row by a separating dot only in same size and in same type. The location determined for the group by the metallic apples asymmetrically flowing. The diagonal composition can only be balance by placing the lettering on top right, which creates a hidden diagonal among the biggest apple on front-left.

The attitude about the sizes of the types for the whole *Black music market* set with its single releases is different than the rest of the sleeves. The letters are bigger, bolder, and placed in a surface which filled by them almost. While it is assumed that bigger lettering is more legible and visible, being this bold and this tight filling in a limited space, makes the design more illegible and perceivable visually as a whole.

Not only background value changed, the point of view also changed by rising and getting far. The grey scale, which represents the millions of tones correspond independent from their hue, changed deeply so no apple can be perceived as a whole apple by the viewer. This made by reducing the number of different grey tones and increasing the areas other grey tones, black, which is the most increased one, and white. The new grey scale obtained let the objects / apples perceived smaller in size and make both the whole surface and letters more legible. Being white on black surface makes the letters perceived thinner with the help of the bigger space surrounding. It is because of a simple visual perception rule about dark / light shapes surrounding by other dark / lights.

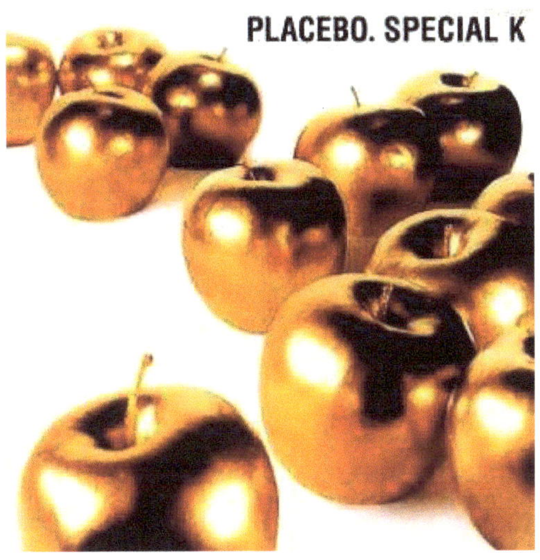

Figure 46. Special k part 1 of 2 release cover, *Author's collection*

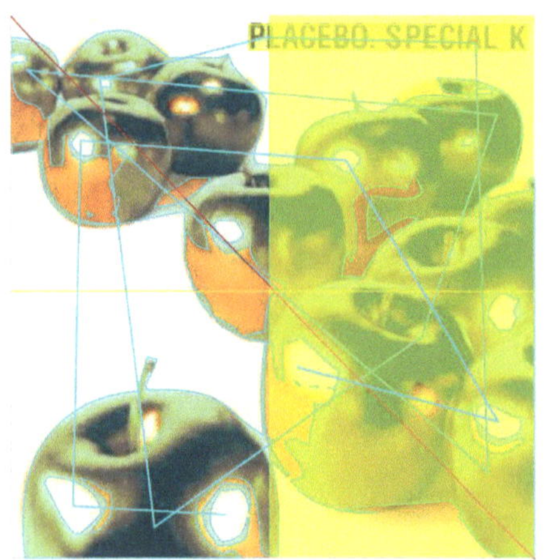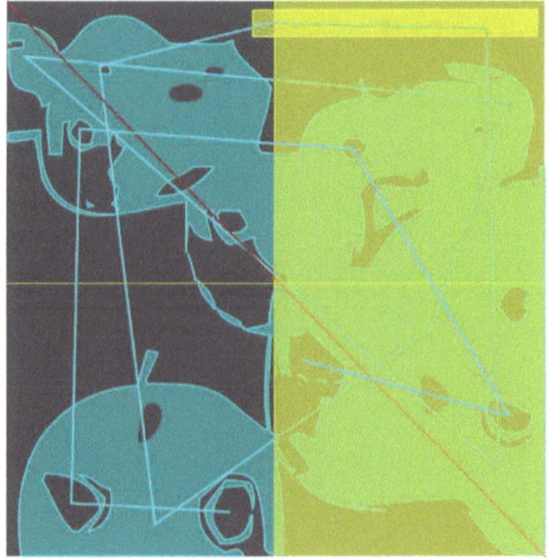

Figure 47. Special k part 1 of 2 release cover's formal analysis, *by Seker*

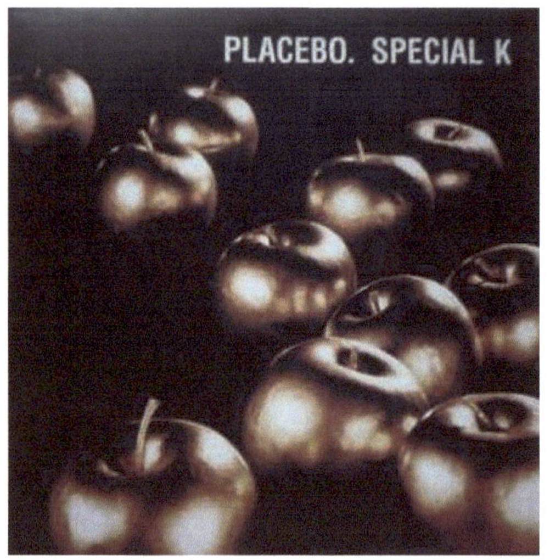

Figure 48. Special k part 2 of 2 release cover, *Author's collection*

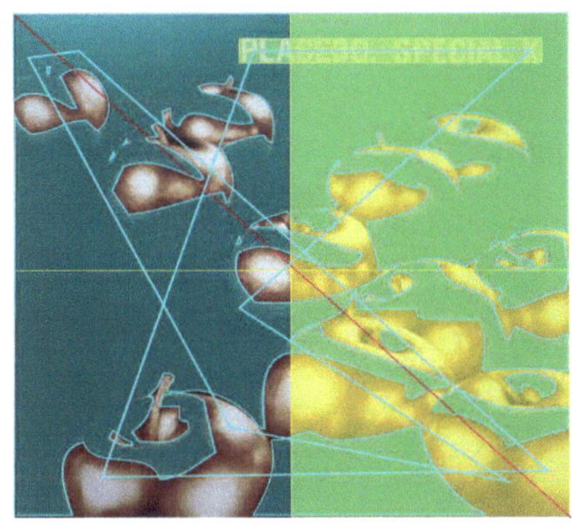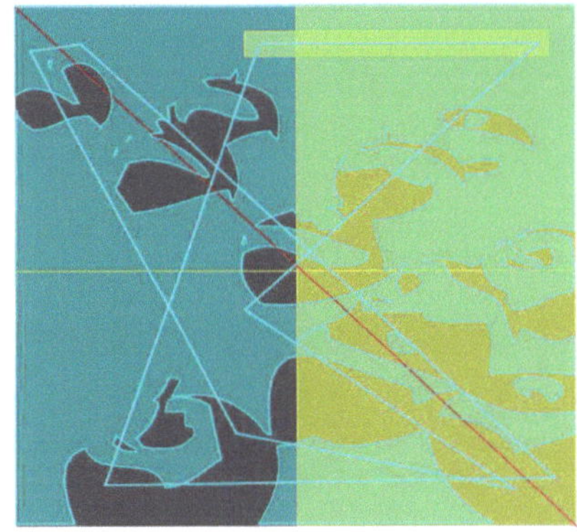

Figure 49. Special k part 2 of 2 release cover's formal analysis, *by Seker*

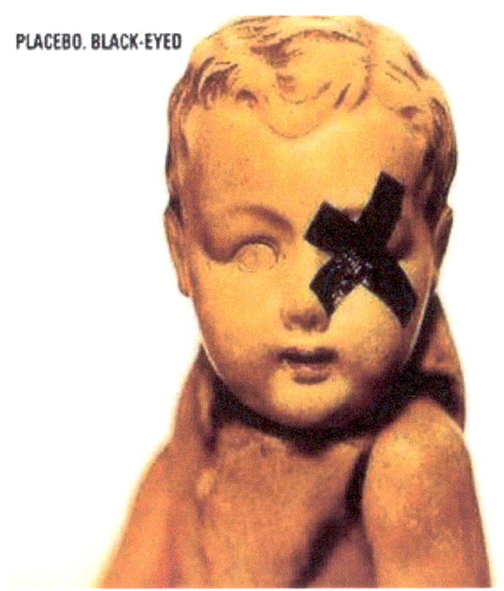

Figure 50. Black-eyed release cover, *Author's collection*

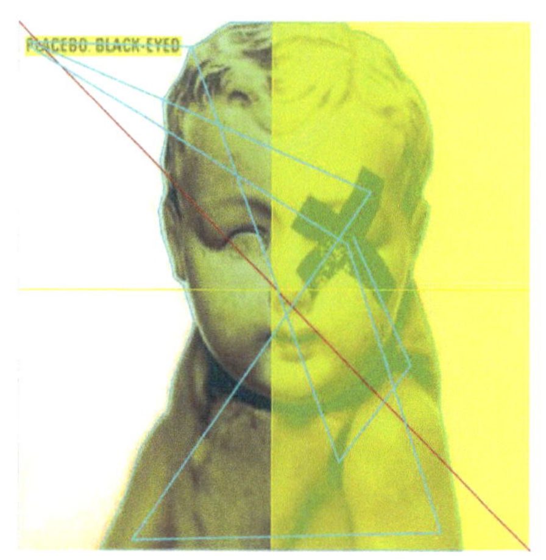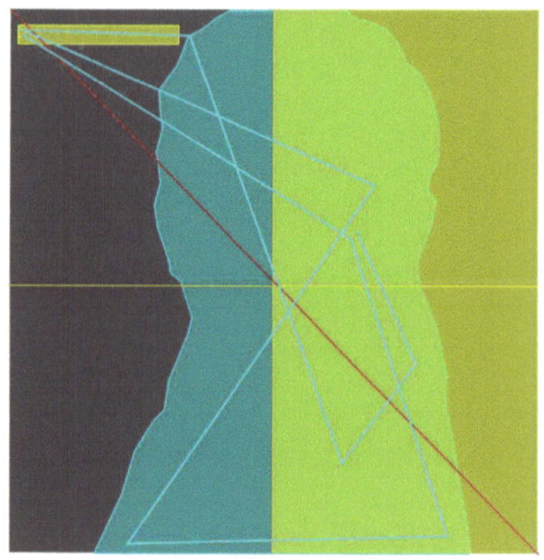

Figure 51 - Black-eyed release cover's formal analysis, *by Seker*

The main composition kept same: there are still two opposing diagonals and asymmetrically balanced composition created by apples and typographic elements as figures. Whether is it black on white as generally presumed as figure, or white on black as holes in the ground because of the visual perception rules are both figures positive or negative in visual design theory. While creating compositions the two opposite dark or light treated as the same, because although they are different, the relation they have or created with the other end is the same.

Labeled as alternative rock, *Black-eyed* is the fourth single release from *Black market music* album dated October 2001 as a one version form (Gregory, 2002: 110). Two versions of the name given song *Black-eyed* and *Pure morning* are the track listing. *Black-eyed* is a song based on the story of a dark and problematic childhood accompanied wailed choruses between mellowed guitars and drums. On the sleeve a male vintage baby doll is representing the drama with its black X marked left eye. Like as in the whole sleeve set of the *Black market music*, the color scheme based on monochromatic neutrals. Black-eyed male baby doll photographed as a portrait looking towards the viewer by sitting sideways. His naked body suits with the nudity canon, which also will continue also after 2000s' sleeve arts of the band. Old and thorn doll has marks and scratches on indicating that it was initially painted. The unidentified body parts with the help of wavy hair creates a movement balanced with the bold straightness of the X shaped bandage in its eye. The bandage with its blackness suits very well with the lettering used to write the name of the release and the band: both are straight and bold without curvy endings or changing line widths except the main characteristics of the letters.

The portrait placed in the slight right of the design surface's center so that the X shaped bands placed just on the vertical right golden section of the square 1:1 and on the upper right focal point determined by intersecting with the horizontal golden section over the horizon. The focal points of the design areas are the most attractive and effective locations for some elements to perceived immediately (Landa, 2019: 160-161). They help to organize the surface, sending the messages accurately and hierarchically. From the bold X shape the coloring system leads the eye to the typographic elements, which are also black and let them to be red. White background, which creates a gap leads the viewer eye to come back to the doll as an entity, a figure to examine visually. The body and the huge – unproportionally big head of the baby doll asymmetrically balance the small but detailed typography on top left side. A dynamism created by three only elements and neutral color scheme reflects the success of the design of the sleeve: a baby doll, black & white.

Epilogue

The 25 officially released sleeves of the band *Placebo* examined visually by getting help from what they are presenting from inside: music. As a service discipline, graphic design work countless sectors like music industry in this instance. When the sleeves examined, it is easily found out that after debut releases, although slightly changes in record company and designers occurred, a general visual concept applied. Among the characteristics of this concept, color schemes chosen, composition, balance types, typography, photography, and visual effects applied are similar. While neutral color schemes used with a little touch of color, the compositions which are open and asymmetrically balanced diagonally. The photographic techniques and subjects chosen related to each other both as form and content. The visual effects as approaches are similar. And finally, typographic elements and styles are almost the same, which creates a great deal of continuity and unity among the whole set.

References

Arnheim, R. (1974). Art and Visual Perception: Psychology of the Creative Eye: 50th Anniversary Printing. Berkeley: University of California Press.

Berger, H.M. (2011). Metal, Rock, and Jazz: Perception and Phenomenology of Musical Experience. Hanover: Wesleyan University Press.

Bleicher, S. (2012). Contemporary Color: Theory and Use. Clifton Park: Cengage Learning.

Buckley, P. (2003). The Rough Guide to Rock: The Definitive Guide to More than 1200 Artists and Bands. London: Rough Guides.

Cogan, B. (2006). Encyclopedia of Punk Music and Culture. Westport: Greenwood Press.

Darman, P. (Ed.). (2013). World War II: The Holocaust and Life Under Nazi Occupation. New York: Rosen Publishing.

De Barres, P. (1996). Rock Bottom: Dark Moments in Music Babylon. New York: St. Martin's Press.

Dimery, R. & Rodeia, K. (2020). Cult Musicians: 50 Progressive Performers You Need to Know. London: Quatro Knows.

Droste, M. (2002). Bauhaus: 1919-1933. Köln: Taschen.

Ellis, I. (2012). Brit Wits: A History of British Rock Humor. Bristol: Intellect Books.

Feisner, E.A. (2006). Colour: How to Use Colour in Art and Design: Second Edition. London: Laurence King Publishing.

Fielder, H. (2013). Pink Floyd: Behind the Wall: The Complete Psychedelic History from 1965 to Today New York: Race Point Publishing.

Finger, S., Zaidel, D.W., Boller, F. & Bogousslavsky, J. (Eds.). (2001). The Fine Arts, Neurology, and Neuroscience: New Discoveries and Changing Landscapes: Progress in Brain Research. Amsterdam: Elsevier.

Geffen, S. (2020). Glitter Up the Dark: How Pop Music Broke the Binary. Austin: University of Texas Press.

Goddard, S. (2009) Mozipedia: The Encyclopedia of Morrisey and the Smiths. London: Random House.

Gregory, A. (2002) The International Who's Who in Popular Music. London: Europa Publishing.

Griffing, S.L. (2007) The Golden Section: An Ancient Egyptian and Grecian Proportion. Bloomington: Xlibris Publishing.

Gulla, B. (2006) The Greenwood Encyclopedia of Rock History: The Grunge and Post-grunge Years, 1991-2005. Westport: Greenwood Press.

Harmon, V. (2013). Painting in Acrylic: Artist's Library Series. Irvine: Walter Foster Publishing.

Harter, N. (2006). Clearings in the Forest: On the Study of Leadership. West Lafayette: Purdue University Press.

Hoskyns, B. (2003). Ragged Glories: City Lights, Country Funk, American Music. Toronto: Pilmico.

Hawkins, S. (2017). The British Pop Dandy: Masculinity, Popular Music and Culture. Oxon: Routledge.

Heller, S. & Fernandes, T. (2010). Becoming a Graphic Designer: A Guide to Careers in Design. Hoboken: John Wiley & Sons.

Henderson, D. (2001). The Beatles Uncovered: 1,000,000 Mob-Top Murders by the Fans and the Famous. Tampa: Black Book Company.

Holzschlag, M.E. (2003). Color for Websites. Sea Cliff: RotoVision.

Landa, R. (2014). The Essential Graphic Design Solutions: 5th Edition. Boston: Cengage Learning.

Landa, R. (2019). The Essential Graphic Design Solutions: 6th Edition. Boston: Cengage Learning.

Larkin, C. (2000). The Virgin Encyclopedia of Nineties Music. London: Virgin Publishing.

Larkin, C. (2011). The Encyclopedia of Popular Music. London: Omnibus Press.

Lauer, D.A. & Pentak, S. (2016). Design Basics: Ninth Edition. Boston: Cengage Learning.

Lime, H. (2019). The Smiths. Morrisville: lulu.com.

Meggs, P.B. & Purvis, A.W. (2016). Meggs' History of Graphic Design. Hoboken: Wiley.

Morton Jr, D.L. (2004). Sound Recording: The Lifestory of a Technology. Baltimore: John Hopkins University Press.

Murphy, D. (2009). Designing for the King: From Chaos to Order by Designing Within. Mustang: Tate Publishing.

Neret, G. (2015). Klimt. Los Angeles: Taschen.

Nuit, N.P. (2015). Chanting Mantras: Guide to Chanting Mantras with Best Chords. Gzira: AoL.

Poulin, R. (2012). The Language of Graphic Design. Beverly: Rockport Publishers.

Ramakers, R. (2002). Less + More: Droog Design in Context. Rotterdam: 010 Publishers.

Ramirez, L.R. (2013). Design Principles and Methods for Composing Artwork. Bloomington: iUniverse.

Rhyne, M.T. (2016). Applying Color Theory to Digital Media and Visualization. Boca Raton: CRC Press.

Shaffer, T.S. & Shaffer, D. (2019). Metaphor: The Universal Language of Photgraphy: A Search for Meaning. Indianapolis: Dog Ear Publishing.

Shapiro, A.G. & Todorovic, D. (Eds.). (2017). The Oxford Compendium of Visual Illusions. New York: Oxford University Press.

Shepherd, J., Horn, D., Laing, D., Oliver, P. & Wicke, P. (Eds.). (2003). Continuum Encyclopedia of Popular Music of the World: Volume I: Media, Industry and Society. London: Continuum.

Sherin, A. (2013). Design Elements, Using Images to Create Graphic Impact: A Graphic Style Manual for Effective Image Solutions in Graphic Design. Beverly: Rockport Publishers.

Sonak, S.M. (2017). Marine Shells of Goa: A Guide to Identification. Cham: Springer.

Squire, V., Forssman, F. & Willberg, H.P. (2006). Getting It Right with Type. London: Laurence King Publishing.

Stanton, S. (2003). The Tombstone Tourist: Musicians: 2nd Edition. New York: Pocket Books.

Strong, M.C. (1998). The Great Rock Discography. London: Canongate.

Talevski, N. (2006). Rock Obituaries: Knocking on Heaven's Door. London: Omnibus Press.

Thompson, D. (2010). Hello Spaceboy: The Rebirth of David Bowie. Toronto: ECW Press.

Valentine, C. (2017). The Chick and the Dead: Life and Death Behind Mortuary Doors. New York: St. Martin's.

Wheiss-Stauffacher, H. (1974). The Marvelous World of Music Machines: Volume 9. Bunkyo: Kodansha.

Whitbread, D. (2001). The Design Manual. Sydney: UNSW Press.

Whitburn, J. (1999). Joel Whitburn's 1998 Billboard Music Yearbook. Gold River: Record Research, Inc.

Wild, P. (Ed.). (2009). Please: Fiction Inspired by the Smiths. New York: Harper Perennial.

Wiseman-Trowse, N. (2013). Nick Drake: Dreaming England. London: Reaktion Books.

Wong, W. (1972). Principles of Two-Dimensional Design. New York: John Wiley and Sons.

Internet Referencing

https://www.allmusic.com/artist/placebo-mn0000355412/discography. Retrieved 11 May 2020.

https://www.allmusic.com/album/taste-in-men-mw0001891754. Retrieved 01 January 2019.

https://www.amazon.com/Special-K-Slave-Wage-Johnny/dp/B000056MKO. Retrieved 03 February 2020.

https://www.amazon.es/Slave-Wage-Placebo/dp/B00004Y9RV. Retrieved 16 June 2020.

https://www.discogs.com/Placebo-Burger-Queen-Fran%C3%A7ais/release/7939664. Retrieved 21 August 2019.

https://www.discogs.com/Placebo-Come-Home/master/164634. Retrieved 25 January 2019.

https://www.discogs.com/Placebo-Every-You-Every-Me/release/214091. Retrieved 31 April 2020.

https://www.nme.com/photos/the-smiths-the-stories-behind-all-27-of-their-provocative-album-and-single-sleeves-1424816. Retrieved 08 June 2019.

https://themmf.net/2015/03/27/artist-and-manager-awards-2015-sponsored-by-dice-the-winners/. Retrieved 30 August 2020.

http://traductionsetparoles.over-blog.com/article-15983014.html. Retrieved 17 March 2020.

http://www.trouserpress.com/entry.php?a= placebo. Retrieved 26 March 2019.

https://www.vice.com/en_uk/article/3bkk98/rank-your-records-brian-molko-skeptically-rates-placebos-eight-lps. Retrieved 13 May 2019.

Table of Contents